Our Adoption

To Muriel
May th

~~~ ✗

Our Adoption
As Sons

Sealed in the Courts of Heaven

by

Mo Tizzard

STOREHOUSE BOOKS

EASTBOURNE

STOREHOUSE
BOOKS

ISBN – 978-0-9566249-4-9

Published by
STOREHOUSE BOOKS
19 Trossachs Close, Eastbourne,
BN23 8HA, England
Email: storehousebooks@sky.com

Cover Design by Helen Owen Marketing
Enterprises (HOME) CIC
www.homecic.com

Acknowledgements

Many thanks go to my dear friend Hazel Munn, who has so painstakingly proof read this book. She went beyond the call of duty as I revised and added to so many chapters and sections. All the way through she has encouraged me, prayed for me and for this book. Plus she has helped me see the relevance of all that I have written. Bless you Hazel.

Thanks also goes to Richard Harland at Helen Owen Marketing Enterprises (HOME) for his design skills.

Finally thanks to my husband Bill who spots those little things that I miss; and who has faithfully prayed this book into fruition.

Contents

Introduction

Having unsuccessfully tried to have a second child, our friends decided to adopt. They went through all the legal channels, and having been told there wasn't much chance of their being able to adopt a young baby, they happily agreed to adopt a toddler. The paperwork was completed and the adoption was officially recognised and ratified in court. The toddler, who had spent most of his young life in a foster home, became a member of their family just a few months before his second birthday.

In the eyes of the law, both their sons were officially recognised as being their children. The youngest had been legally adopted into their family and his adoption was officially registered with the representative court of the land. Whereas the eldest had been born into their family and his birth was registered, according to law at the local registry office. The youngest son is now growing up with the knowledge that he was adopted; that he was chosen by his parents to be a loved and wanted member of their family. But the eldest son knows that he didn't need to be adopted by his parents. Because he had been born by natural birth into their family. The youngest son is a loved and cherished member of the family - through adoption; and the eldest son is a loved and cherished member of their family - through natural birth.

Have you ever wondered why believers who have been born again, who have been given new life by the Spirit of God, are told that they have been adopted into the Father's family? As shown by the illustration above, if someone has been born into a family surely they don't then need to be adopted by that same family? But so many times those who have experienced the new birth, that is described in chapter three of John's gospel, are told that they have been chosen by our Heavenly Father to be adopted as a loved and wanted member of His family. This has always puzzled me and made me question, "Why do we need to be both born again and adopted into the same family by the same Father?" Or to put it another way "Why do we need to be adopted into the same family that we have already been born into?" This question prompted me to do some research on what 'receiving adoption' or 'receiving the adoption as sons' actually means, as spoken of in scripture.

As I researched, I wasn't surprised to discover that being adopted in the context and culture that we know today, is totally different from the adoption that was written about in the Bible. It isn't referring to our Heavenly Father adopting us into His family in the same way that children who need parents are adopted. It isn't referring to our Father adopting us as orphans needing shelter and care. The adoption that is written about in scripture is in fact an acknowledgement of our abilities - and the potential we have within us. Receiving the adoption as sons isn't referring to the adoption of children at all. It is an adoption that referred to what happened when a young man reached adulthood in the culture of that time. Having said that please note that in scripture, this adoption in no way excludes, or is detrimental, to women. In fact when Paul wrote about receiving adoption as sons in his letters to the early churches, they knew exactly what he was saying; and his words would have blown their minds. My prayer is that as you read on and understand what was, and is being said about receiving the adoption as sons, the full truth of Paul's words will impact your mind and your heart in that same way too.

NB: I have highlighted some words by using italics, both in the scriptures and in what I've written personally. I've done this for reasons of clarity, so that you can understand what is being said more easily.

Chapter One

Born From Above

It was Jesus Himself that told us that we must be born again; and the conversation that brought this about is recorded in John's gospel.   John is spoken of as the disciple that Jesus loved - not directly by name, but by implication (John 19:26). The phrase, 'the one that Jesus loved' is found in several verses in scripture. But all those verses are only in the gospel that John wrote, which always makes me smile.   I'm sure Jesus loved all His disciples equally, but there were three disciples that seemed closer to Him than the others - Peter, James and John.   We only know this because these three disciples were privileged to be with Jesus at certain special moments. Not surprisingly it is in John's gospel that we are told of many of the personal encounters that took place in Jesus life, perhaps more than the other three gospels - because John was actually there to witness them. One of those encounters was with a very curious Pharisee called Nicodemus.

Nicodemus had seen the signs that Jesus was performing among the people and he wanted to clarify what he had already observed for himself - that God was with Him.   But Nicodemus needed to meet Jesus 'on the quiet', out of the public gaze; and definitely without his fellow members of the Sanhedrin knowing. They were very angry with Jesus and wanted to discredit Him; so they certainly wouldn't have approved of Nicodemus, one of their own, meeting with Him. So he went to see Jesus at night, which was a very risky thing to do. Because without adequate lighting, night time was when thieves and robbers plied their trade. But Nicodemus was prepared to risk it in order to meet this amazing 'Man'.

'Now there was a Pharisee, a man named Nicodemus who was a member of the Jewish ruling council.
He came to Jesus at night and said, "Rabbi, we know that you are a teacher who has come from God. For no one could perform the signs you are doing if God were not with him."
Jesus replied, "Very truly I tell you, no one can see the kingdom of God unless they are born again."' John 3:1-3

Jesus reply to Nicodemus statement of belief starts with 'Very truly' in this NIV version of the Bible. In other versions these two words have been translated as 'Most assuredly' or 'Truly truly'. But in looking at the original words, before any translations were made, it seems that Jesus was actually saying, 'Amen amen'.

NB: It's helpful to know that when we read the same word written twice together in scripture, it is so that we will pay close attention to it. Because the repetition of the same word means it has twice the importance. Jesus did this quite often to emphasise what He was saying; and to make His listener(s) sit up and take note. However this is not always so obvious in our modern translations, because they have replaced the first of the repeated words, i.e. 'very truly' instead of 'truly truly'. This is understandable in this day and age, because without most people knowing the importance of repeating the same word, using a word like 'very' allowed the translators to make clear the importance of that word.

The word amen comes from the Hebrew word '*amen*; which springs from the almost identical word '*aman*, which means 'believe' or 'faithful'. Therefore to say amen at the end of a prayer is not just a statement of agreement. Amen is rooted in a statement of belief that what has been said is true. It is an expression of absolute trust and confidence in something. To say amen is to make what someone else has said, truly your own. According to my lexicon amen is a remarkable word. It is remarkable because during the process of the scriptures being translated from the Hebrew language into the Greek; then from Greek into Latin; and then from Latin being translated into many other languages - the word amen survived without being changed at all. In fact amen has been called the best known word in human speech!

Jesus response of 'Very truly' or 'Amen amen' is an acknowledgement that Nicodemus' assessment that God is with Him is correct, faithful and true. Sensing that Nicodemus is near, Jesus goes on to explain how he can enter into God's kingdom - by being born again; and by emphasising that there is no other way - 'no-one can see the kingdom of God unless they are born again.'. Although the word 'see' here can mean 'to see with the eyes'; it also means 'to see with the mind, to perceive, to know', 'to become acquainted with by experience'. But it's not an experience that Nicodemus could comprehend. In fact Jesus statement leaves Nicodemus totally perplexed. So he asks the question....

'"How can someone be born when they are old? Nicodemus asked "Surely they cannot enter a second time into their mother's womb to be born!"
Jesus answered, "Very truly I tell you, no one can enter the kingdom of God unless they are born of water and the Spirit.
Flesh gives birth to flesh, but the Spirit gives birth to spirit."' John 3:4-6

Nicodemus, being a Pharisee was used to debating points of the Law. By putting the point that it was impossible to enter his mother's womb a second time, was his way of excluding the impossible, in order to find out exactly what Jesus meant about being born again. Again Jesus agrees, 'Amen amen', that Nicodemus is right in what he's saying - 'no one can enter a second time into their mother's womb'. He then informs Nicodemus that this second birth is a spiritual birth. It's nothing to do with a natural birth; it has nothing to do with the flesh. This second birth occurs only when the Holy Spirit of God gives birth to someone's spirit. This is difficult for us earthlings to understand, but it helps if we know what the original words 'born again' mean.

The word 'born' in the original Greek is *gennao*, which means exactly that - 'to be born' or 'to be begotten'. It's the word that's used at the beginning of Matthew's gospel when he tells us about Jesus' genealogy - 'Abraham was the father of Isaac, Isaac was the father of Jacob....' (Matthew 1:2) In the original Greek it says - 'Abraham *gennao* Isaac, Isaac *gennao* Jacob...' and on down the holy line. This shows us that the word 'born' that Jesus is using here means 'to be fathered'.

The second word 'again' is the Greek word *anothen*, which has a few meanings, which are - 'from above', 'from a higher place', 'from the first', 'from the beginning', 'anew' or 'over again'. If we apply all these meanings it will give us far more understanding of what exactly Jesus is saying to Nicodemus -

"No one can see the kingdom of God unless they are born from above."
"No one can see the kingdom of God unless they are born from a higher place."
"No one can see the kingdom of God unless they are born anew."
"No one can see the kingdom of God unless they are born over again."

If we also apply the word 'fathered' in the place of 'born' when looking at the first word *gennao* then we can see even more in the above phrases, as follows -

"No one can see the kingdom of God unless they are Fathered from above."
"No one can see the kingdom of God unless they are Fathered from a higher place."
"No one can see the kingdom of God unless they are Fathered anew."
"No one can see the kingdom of God unless they are Fathered over again."

We aren't told, but it seems that Nicodemus took Jesus' words to heart. Because later on we read of him endeavouring to get the chief priests and his fellow Pharisees to at least listen to Jesus rather than just condemning Him outright - 'Does our law condemn a man without first hearing him to find out what he's been doing.' (John 7:50). But the real confirmation of

Nicodemus receiving and acting upon Jesus' words about being born again is seen in chapter nineteen of John's gospel. Joseph of Arimathea had asked, and received permission from Pilate to take Jesus' body away for burial after the crucifixion; and we are told that -

'He was accompanied by Nicodemus, the man who earlier had visited Jesus at night. Nicodemus brought a mixture of myrrh and aloes, about seventy-five pounds. Taking Jesus' body, the two of them wrapped it, with spices, in strips of linen. This was in accordance with Jewish burial customs.' (John 19:39-40).

What an honour this was for the man who had not let his position as a Pharisee, stop him from seeking out the truth of who Jesus was. It all came about because he didn't let others in the same position stop him, even if it meant he had to go to see Jesus by night. His reward, and ours, was that Jesus revealed to him the foundational truth that no one can see the kingdom of God unless they are born again, born from above by the Holy Spirit.

A Way of Life

This foundation truth had quite an impact on John because when he began to write his gospel, one of the first things he told his readers was - 'Yet to all who did receive him, to those who believed in his name, he gave the right to become children of God - children born not of natural descent, nor of human decision or a husband's will, but born of God.' (John 1:12-13). It was a truth that John re-iterated in several places in his first letter. He told them...

'If you know that he is righteous, you know that everyone who does what is right has been born of him.' 1 John 2:29

'No one who is born of God will continue to sin, because God's seed remains in them; they cannot go on sinning, because they have been born of God.' 1 John 5:18

John wanted his readers to understand that being born again was more than just an experience - it was a way of life. That being 'born from above' or 'Fathered from above' imparted an understanding on the inside of us of right and wrong. We may call it conscience or intuition, but it is God given so that we can choose how to behave without consulting a rule book. Being born again gives true believers a desire not to sin. I'm sure I can say that, even though believers do make mistakes from time to time, sinning is not something we set out to do intentionally. It's not in our DNA to deliberately grieve the Holy Spirit of God (Ephesians 4:30) who dwells within us. Another wonderful consequence of being a born again child of our heavenly Father is the love that He gives us; and that He pours through us to others, especially our brothers and sisters in Christ, who have also been born into His family.

'Dear friends, let us love one another, for love comes from God. Everyone who loves has been born of God and knows God.' 1 John 4:7

'Everyone who believes that Jesus is the Christ is born of God, and everyone who loves the father loves his child as well.' 1 John 5:1

Our status as His child also gives us more than love, conscience and intuition, it gives us confidence. A confidence that is built on our faith in a loving caring God and Father. A confidence that we can call on His help to overcome the difficulties we face in life. Not a guaranteed avoidance of difficulties, but a knowledge that He will be there with us in anything we may go through. As His child He has promised that whatever we go through, do or encounter will not separate us from His love - 'Who shall separate us from the love of Christ? Shall trouble or hardship or persecution or famine or nakedness or danger or sword? (Romans 8:35).

'... for everyone born of God overcomes the world. This is the victory that has overcome the world, even our faith.' 1 John 5:4

John isn't the only one to speak of being born again. Although those actual words aren't used, the Apostle Paul in his letter to the Galatians confirms the difference in being born of the flesh and being born of the Spirit. He likens our new birth to the birth of Isaac, when he says of Abraham's sons that Ishmael was born of the flesh, whereas Isaac was born by the power of the Spirit.

'Now you, brothers and sisters, like Isaac, are children of promise. At that time the son born according to the flesh persecuted the son born by the power of the Spirit. It is the same now.' Galatians 4:28-29

It's clear that Isaac wasn't born because of Abraham and Sarah's flesh, they had certainly tried that and it hadn't happened (Genesis 15:3). Isaac, in fact was born despite their flesh. His birth was a miraculous gift of God, because when he arrived Abraham was 100 years old and Sarah was 90 years old and well past childbearing age. Isaac came to birth because God had made Abraham a promise; and we too as believers, have been born again by the power of the Spirit, born again because of God's promise. God's promise, which is - 'Yet to all those who did receive him, to those who believed in his name, he gave the right to become children of God.' (John 1:12).

Being Born Again

'Praise be to the God and Father of our Lord Jesus Christ! In his great mercy he has given us new birth into a living hope through the resurrection of Jesus Christ from the dead, and into an inheritance that can never perish, spoil or fade. This inheritance is kept in heaven for you,' 1 Peter 1:3-4

For all true believers the journey to the point of being born again is an individual experience. As a midwife once said, 'No two births are ever the same', and similarly no two 'second births' are ever the same. For some there is a deep longing to know who He is, which has built up over several encounters with His people and His presence. Some have discovered who He is, and what He has done for us, through reading His Word. For others there is a one off revelation that opens up their heart to respond and acknowledge Him as their Saviour. For others there is a slow journey of understanding that culminates in an uncompromising acknowledgement that He is not only the Saviour of mankind, but that He is their own personal Saviour. All these routes, all these journeys to understanding, plus untold others that are unique to individuals, have culminated in our receiving Jesus as our Saviour. But the common denominator for all of us is that at some point in the journey we have become aware of our sinfulness, repented of it and received His forgiveness. A forgiveness that was, and is based purely on what Jesus did for us on the cross, as the perfect sacrifice for sin.

For me, the awareness of my sinfulness came in waves. I didn't call it 'my sinfulness' I just remember getting to the point of thinking, that I was so bad that even if I emigrated I wouldn't be able to get away from me - I would be still be taking me with me! However the understanding of what sin was, and the repentance of my sin in particular, didn't occur until later, after I had received the revelation that God was actually real.

As a non church person I had been persuaded by a new friend to go to monthly ladies meetings that were being held on a Monday evening at her church. Through those monthly meetings and the prayers of the ladies of that church, I was slowly but surely drawn towards a deeper desire to know if God existed. But it wasn't until four young people from another church came to speak one January evening that I really began to sit up and take notice. One by one each young person testified to their belief in God; and their combined testimonies certainly got my attention.

The last one to speak that evening was a young man called Robert. He told us that he had messed up earlier that day and was so full of sorrow that he done wrong; but how overjoyed he was that God had forgiven him. He was so full of the joy of forgiveness and the goodness of God that I thought to myself, 'If I touched him, it would be like touching a hot line to God!' Then to my surprise, when Robert finished speaking he said, "Let's pray now, because I believe there is somebody here who wants to get through to God".

As it happened I was sitting in the front row that evening, as it had been the only seat left that had been available to me. To my dismay I saw that Robert was looking over my head. He was looking at all those that were seated behind me, as he searched for who that person might be. 'Oh no!' I thought, 'he doesn't know it's me that wants to get through to God!' Everyone closed their eyes to pray, but instead of praying I was just crying out inside of me, "It's me! It's me!" That's when I heard a rushing noise in my ears, my heart started thumping, tears streamed down my face and, as the others were praying, I sat there watching my knees shake!   'I must be ill', I thought, 'I've got the flu!'. But the next day, when I eventually told my friend what had happened, she surprised me by saying that I'd been born again - that I was now a child of God!

The minister's wife came round later that day, and after having asked me what happened she said, "Have you repented dear?" I hadn't realised that I should have repented. I had just responded with a strong desire to know Him when the invitation to pray came; and had been rewarded with the touch of His Spirit on my life. So I told her that I hadn't. The minister's wife then led me in a prayer of repentance and I repeated the appropriate words after her.

At the time, I repeated those words of repentance in all sincerity, and I accepted that I was forgiven - because I was. But it wasn't until a few weeks later that I really knew and appreciated how wonderful the Lord's forgiveness is. I had always tried to be a 'good girl' as a child; it was my way of receiving acceptance from my parents and others. The desire to get away from 'me' before my salvation had been real and unsettling; but I wasn't aware of the depth of my sinfulness at that point, or after I had first been 'born again'. However, as I read more and more scripture over the weeks the full revelation of my sinfulness hit me hard and what followed was a deeper repentance. That repentance was quickly followed by a sweet sense of His presence and the joy of His forgiveness. It was only then that I realised that He had chosen to save me, despite knowing all about the wrong stuff I'd done and the wrong attitudes I'd had. He hadn't accepted me because I was a 'good girl', which I discovered was a subconscious thought that had to surface before I could recognise it for what it was. It was because of His grace, and only His grace that I was now His child. My salvation was a gift from Him to me. It was all down to His unconditional love that I had been born again.

That was over forty years ago and I realised quite quickly that my born again experience was far more dramatic than many true believers have had. I think this was because my husband reacted really strongly against my becoming a Christian; and that experience helped to anchor me in Christ while he continually expressed his disapproval. Interestingly he didn't have any kind of experience when he finally accepted Jesus as His Saviour. But if you want to know the full story and what happened to bring him to that point, you can read about it in my first book, 'How to Pray When he Doesn't Believe'.

There are more ways than can be described as to how people come to that place of receiving Christ; and it's a joy to hear people's testimonies. But whether their salvation culminated in a particular born again experience, or it was a different kind of journey that brought them to that place, the bottom line is...

'If you declare with your mouth, "Jesus is Lord," and believe in your heart that God raised him from the dead, you will be saved. For it is with your heart that you believe and are justified, and it is with your mouth that you profess your faith and are saved.' Romans 10:9-10

When the Holy Spirit breathes life into a man's spirit a new life, a spiritual life is possible. A new life lived in relationship with God, a life that was originally intended for man - right from the very beginning.

Chapter Two

Adoption to Sonship

Having established that we need to be born again. That we need to have the breath of life and relationship breathed into us by the Holy Spirit. We can now look at why scripture talks about our receiving adoption to sonship.

'... He predestined us for *adoption to sonship* by Jesus Christ to Himself, according to the good pleasure of His will' Ephesians 1:5

As I said in the introduction, most people in our modern age don't understand what scripture is actually saying with reference to our adoption. Most people naturally assume that adoption is referring to our Heavenly Father adopting us into His family, in the same way that a couple adopts a baby or a child; thus making that child a legal and permanent member of their family. But scripture was written to a people living in a different time, with a different understanding of what adoption meant. The people that the scriptures were originally written for knew exactly what was being referred to when they read about adoption. It was a different kind of legal status all together. Biblical adoption refers, not to young children, but to sonship and being an heir of the Father, which is totally different from our modern day understanding of it.

'... that we might receive the *adoption as sons*' Galatians 4:5 (NKJV)

'... the Spirit you received brought about your *adoption to sonship*. And by Him we cry out, "*Abba*, Father." Romans 8:15

'In love he predestined us for adoption to sonship through Jesus Christ, in accordance with his pleasure and will' Ephesians 1:5

Some may find it difficult that adoption in the New Testament is always linked and equated with sons or sonship. Difficult because these scriptures don't include the words daughters or mention women. But as we look deeper into this subject we will find that they in no way exclude the fairer sex. Far from it. Once we understand what was meant by adoption in the Bible, the desire to change or add to the wording of these verses - in order to make them 'fair' to the 'fairer sex' - will soon disappear.

Let's Take a Look at the Romans

The best way to begin understanding what adoption as sons actually means in scripture is to look at what it meant to those who originally received Paul's letters. Those who had received the good news of the gospel and had given their lives to Christ. Those who had joined together in local areas united through their love of Jesus; and who had become known as the early churches. These early churches were all situated in cities that were at that time under the control of the Roman Empire.

Paul wrote letters to all these churches, instructing them in the mysteries and joys of being children of God; and his letters were passed from one church to another; from one area of the Roman Empire to another. Paul realised that as Gentiles they wouldn't know anything about the Jewish scriptures. That they would be more able to understand what he was saying if he illustrated the truths he wanted to get across to them, with what they already knew from living in a Roman culture. A culture that was probably far more well known than their own original cultures, because the Romans had been in charge of their cities, their countries, for around one hundred and fifty years and weren't in a hurry to leave.

History tells us that in the years between 100 BC and 400 AD the city of Rome was the largest city in the world; and it was the capitol of the Roman Empire. The area that comprised the Roman Empire included Southern Europe, Turkey, the Middle East and North Africa, which meant that it completely encircled and surrounded the Mediterranean Sea. Its territory included 48 nations, as we know them now; and it is estimated that Rome and it's Emperor had influence and control over approximately 70 to 100 million people, which was, at that time 21% of the world's entire population.

Those living in the Roman Empire, and especially Roman citizens, had far more social structures and defined stages in their lives than we do now. In order to understand what is meant by adoption we need to look at the defined stages of a child's life in the Roman Empire, which also defined their place in society.

In the time when the New Testament letters were written, a young child was known as a *paidion* - which is exactly what it means - a small child. The education of all young children was under the control of their parents. In the early days the emphasis was on their moral development more than actual education. It was Mum's job to teach them about honesty, self reliance, respect for the law, honour for their gods, and above all unquestioning obedience. Alongside all this, Mum would teach her young children the elementary basics of reading, writing and arithmetic.

Girls in that culture certainly weren't denied formal education, because they had a future responsibility to educate their own young. But as the girls grew up there was a greater emphasis on learning practical skills such as sewing and weaving and how to run a household. That was because girls were married at a young age; and that marriage that would have been arranged ahead of time by a girl's parents.

When a boy was around the age of seven his education from Mum finished. If he was a member of a good family with status he would continue his education under the instruction of a tutor. If his father was a member of society's better classes, the boy would be put under the daily supervision of a trusted servant called a *paidagogos*. This servant was charged with the duty of supervising the boy's life and his moral behaviour. He was authorised to train up the boy using discipline, chastisement and instruction, In fact whatever was necessary to promote the boy's best development. The supervision of the *paidagogos* was such that boy would not be allowed so much as to step out of the house without him. Not, that is until he reached the age of manhood.

If a boy's father was a man of high position in Rome, in addition to his general and moral education he would be educated in the ways of politics and the affairs of state. He would accompany his father and observe how matters of state were conducted first hand. He would also be trained in the use of military weapons, as well as in riding, swimming, wrestling, and boxing. A boy of lower status however, would learn alongside and be apprenticed to, his father in learning his father's trade.

There was no special ceremony to mark a girl's passing into womanhood, but there was for a boy when he reached manhood. It was the most important thing that would happen in his life and it came when he was around the age of fourteen to sixteen. The year depended, not so much on the boy's physical and intellectual development, it depended on what his father decided.

When the father decided the time was right and his son was ready, the father would take his son to the city's forum and present him as an adult and a citizen. This rite of passage was celebrated at the festival of Liberalia, which was equivalent to the Jewish Bar Mitzvah. The boy, would be given a new robe, a new toga to wear called the toga virilis. Up to that point he had worn the toga praetexta, which was a garment worn by both boys and girls. This toga virilis immediately identified him as being a citizen of Rome and it gave him the eligibility to vote, and he was able to make certain decisions regarding His life! He was no longer considered to be a child, no longer a *paidion* - he was now a *teknon*. As a *teknon* he hadn't reached maturity, he was still under tuition, but he was an acknowledged citizen with certain rights of decision making for himself. When he did mature into full manhood in later life he would enter that final stage of manhood, as a *huios* - a fully mature son who was a complete and accomplished representative on behalf his father.

All these stages of a boy/man's life can be found in the New Testament scriptures. One of the references to a young child, a *paidion* is found right at the beginning of the gospel of Matthew. When Herod heard that the Maji were inquiring about the one who had been born, who was King of the Jews -'He sent them to Bethlehem and said, "Go and search carefully for the child *(paidion)*. As soon as you find him, report to me, so that I too may go and worship him." (Matthew 2:8). Later in Matthew's gospel when the disciples asked Jesus who was the greatest in the kingdom of heaven, Jesus called a little child to Him and said, "Truly I tell you, unless you change and become like little children *(paidion)* you will never enter the kingdom of heaven." (Matthew 18:3).

NB: It's worth noting that a more accurate translation of the word 'change', that is used here, would be 'turn around'. This is borne out by the fact that we can find this word translated as 'converted' in other versions of the Bible. The reason for this is that the words 'turn around' are the true meaning of repentance. When we repent, when we 'turn around', turn away from our sins, we are leaving behind our independent lifestyle and are turning towards Him instead. This turning enables us to follow

Him and follow His directions for our lives. What Jesus said to His disciples in this passage was the same thing that He said to Nicodemus but put in a different way. To Nicodemus, Jesus said - "Very truly I tell you, no one can see the kingdom of God unless they are born again." (John 3:3). To His disciples, Jesus said - "Truly I tell you, unless you change (repent) and become like little children (born again as a spiritual child) you will never enter the kingdom of heaven." (Matthew 18:3).

Now let's get back to the stages that are shown in the New Testament as boys develop into men, and see how they were applied.

Below are a couple of examples of well known scriptures that refer to children, as *teknon*, indicating that they are referring to older children, who are still under the guardianship of tutors but who are considered old enough to be accepted as a citizen. The first is found in Matthew 7:11which most of us know as the Sermon on the Mount, which refers to the time when a large crowd had gathered and Jesus went up on a mountainside and had sat down to teach them. The next is found in John 1:12-13 in the opening passage of John's gospel.

"If you, then, though you are evil, know how to give good gifts to your children (*teknon*), how much more will your Father in heaven give good gifts to those who ask Him!" Matthew 7:11

'Yet to all who did receive Him, to those who believed in His name, He gave the right to become children (*teknon*) of God - children (*teknon*) born not of natural descent, nor of human decision or a husband's will, but born of God' John 1:12-13

Looking at the second scripture in a bit more depth it seems that the word 'right' means 'power of choice'; and the word 'become' means to 'come into being'. So when we put this all together we see that the Apostle John is saying - Yet to all who did receive Him, to those who believed in His name, He gave the 'power of choice' to 'come into being' as children (*teknon*) of God. This passage shows us that when we believed in His name we had the power of choice, the right to come into being, to be born from above as children (*teknon*) of God - not as babies or little children - but as those who are recognised as citizens of heaven!

There is another verse in Luke's gospel, which gives us an intriguing insight into the transition of Jesus from being considered a *paidion* to being known as a *teknon*. But I won't share that with you right now, as I'm saving that for later!

The final stage of manhood described in scripture is as being a *huios*. This is the most used word when we read the word son, whether it refers to any man or if it refers to Jesus in particular. A prime example is found right at the beginning of the New Testament - 'This is the genealogy of Jesus the Messiah the son (*huios*) of David, the son (*huios*) of Abraham' (Matthew 1:1).   Jesus is known throughout scripture as the Son (*huios*) of God, for instance when He was being tempted in the wilderness - 'If you are the Son (*huios*) of God....' (Matthew 4:6).

Now that the groundwork has been covered in looking at the stages of boyhood and manhood in the original culture and language, let us look at what adoption as sons meant to the churches and the Christians who were living under Roman rule in the Roman Empire in the first century AD. Because the letters they received then were eventually incorporated into the New Testament and are now known to us as books of the Bible.

Chapter Three

The Reasons for Adoption

There were two main reasons for adoption, which both involve sons - sons who were old enough to be responsible. The first reason for adoption was because in those days there was no welfare state and women didn't work. Therefore it was vitally important for each family to have a son. This was because when a man became too old to work, it was a son's duty to take on all of the family's responsibilities. Society expected him to take over the running of his father's business and to support his elderly parents financially. His wife was expected to take over the running of the household when his mother became too old to oversee or do the household tasks herself. Plus she was responsible for the care and welfare of her in-laws in their old age. Therefore, when it became clear that a couple would not have any children, or they only had daughters and not sons, they would look to adopt someone else's son.

Although he could be younger, this usually took place when that boy was around the age of 14-16 years, when he was considered a *teknon* and had become a citizen of Rome. That was because the primary motivation for an adoption like this was to continue the family line, to take care of the couple in old age and to make sure their family business continued to thrive. Therefore the couple would need to be sure of the character, education and worth of the boy that they were considering for adoption. I would imagine that all these attributes would be well researched so that the couple would have the right son for them, for their household and for their business. It wasn't totally unknown for a childless couple to adopt a child, boy or girl as a *paidion* - a young child or a baby. But the main reason for adoption was not for the protection and care of the child. It was for the benefit of the couple, the household and the family business - and for the continuance of the family line!

The second reason for adoption was not the means of giving a childless couple a son, or providing a son to a couple that only had daughters. The second reason for adoption is that which is referred to when we read in scripture about 'adoption as sons' and our 'adoption to sonship'. This adoption was a legal procedure involving mature adult males, those who had come to the status of being a *huios*.

The Greek word, which is translated as adoption in scripture, is - *huiothesia*, which is actually two words combined together - *huios* & *thesia* - *huios* meaning a son and *thesia* meaning to place in a position.

huios = a son   *thesia* = to place in a position

Therefore the full meaning of adoption spoken of in scripture was when the father of the household officially 'placed' an adult male in the 'position' of being his 'son and heir'.   The son chosen to receive the 'adoption to sonship' was a mature man. He was definitely not a child or paedion and he was not a young man or *teknon*. He was a *huios*, chosen for adoption to sonship and placed in the position of a son when he had reached maturity. The reason for this was because it meant the father could send that mature son to do business on his behalf. The son on his adoption, was placed in a position of authority that guaranteed he would be received and treated in the same way as the father would be treated - just as if he were the father himself.

Now you need to know that this mature son was usually a son of the father and a member of the family..... but not always! If a man adopted his own son, it was the highest honour he could confer on him - *but adoption was not necessarily based on physical birth!* A wise father would adopt as his son and heir whomever he considered to be mentally mature and business savvy; as they would have to carry on the family name and take care of his wealth. If he didn't have any sons or his natural sons were not up to the job, especially if they viewed things from a different perspective than he did, he could adopt another related, or unrelated adult male to be his son and heir.

If he felt it would be preferable, it was even possible for him to adopt a trustworthy servant to be his son and heir. In fact the father could adopt whoever he thought had the wisdom, skill and ability he was looking for in a son and heir. In Roman worldview, sonship did not primarily point backward to the birth of a son into the family; but forward to the inheritance that a father would be passing on. The importance of putting the right person in the position of his son and heir meant a father didn't automatically have to choose a naturally begotten son. He could choose to put another more competent male in that position of sonship - through adoption.

It was the adoption of wise, skilled, able adult males that helped to stabilise and expand the ruling families of Rome and they were key to imperial ideology. Roman Emperors could and did, designate a successor by making them a son by adoption. This way they could pass on the important position of ruling an empire to the one that they felt would do the job well; and in a way that they themselves would like their Empire to be run. Adoption gave them the opportunity to confer rulership to their successor by merit not by heredity.

The Emperor Claudius adopted Nero as his son and heir so that he could succeed him as Emperor. Nero was not a blood relation. Emperor Claudius had a daughter called Octavia, so to make things more acceptable, Nero decided it would be a good idea to marry her. Even though Nero and Octavia weren't blood relations, they were brother and sister in the eyes of the law. So in order for Nero and Octavia to marry, the Roman senate had to pass special legislation to make that marriage legal.

That was because adoption was more than just a ceremony or a custom; it was incorporated into the law. It became a law which could not be reversed. The reason for this law was because it stopped any challenges that a natural son might bring against the right of an adopted son, to an inheritance left to him by their father. Once the son who was chosen for adoption had been through all the legalities, and the ceremony that had finalised his adoption, he remained an heir for as long as he lived. He couldn't be disinherited no matter what he did.

Therefore the father had an important decision to make when deciding who should be considered for adoption. Because all the time the father was still living, the chosen son would act as his representative in any business dealings. And when the father died the son would inherit all or part of the family fortune and the family business. The father could adopt more than one son, and all the above applied in equal shares to them. Therefore the chosen son or sons needed to be someone who could take on the full responsibility of the trust that would be placed in him. Someone who would act as if he were the father himself, in any situation while he was alive and even more importantly when he was no longer around. Someone who would make sure that things were done as the father would have them done, when they had been under his own watchful eye. He needed to choose someone he could confidently 'place in the position a son', place in the position of his *huiothesia*.

The Patria Potestas

Under Roman law every father, as the eldest male member of the household, had absolute power of disposal and control over his family. In legal terms it was called the 'patria potestas' or 'paternal power'. This meant that the father had the power of life and death over every member of his family and his household! Even when a son became a mature adult he still remained under the patria potestas of his father. In fact the son was under his father's power and control for as long as his father lived.

The father could dictate what the son could do or couldn't do, even to the point of making decisions concerning how the son lived - or how he died! The patria potestas guaranteed that the father was obeyed by everyone in his family and in his household without question.   He controlled every aspect of their lives, without exception.   It was a very powerful and a very responsible thing to be in the position of patria potestas.

Therefore if a son, or male member of one household, was chosen to be adopted by the father of another household, to be his son & heir - *it was a very big deal!* This is because that son was under the patria potestas, the power and control, of his own father. So in order to pass out of the absolute control of his natural father and into the equally absolute control of the other father, the son first had to be 'sold'.

The Sale

A formal and legal sale was a necessary process, because without it the transfer of power from one father to another, from one patria potestas to another, would not be legal. The sale, known as the *mancipatio*, applied to the adoption of a son who was considered a *teknon*, by a couple who had no son of their own; and it also applied to the adoption of a grown man, a *huios*, who was to be placed in the position of a son by a new father.

The *mancipatio* was a verbal contract, which took place in the presence of at least five adult witnesses, who had to be Roman citizens and of the age puberty, i.e. a *teknon*. It was used to transfer ownership and it applied not just to the 'emancipating' of children from their natural parents in the transfer of sons from one family to another; it also applied to the transfer of goods, land, animals and slaves.

In the case of adoption, as in any other sale, the adopting father would have in his possession an ingot of copper and there would be someone to hold a pair of copper scales. This was known as the procedure of acquisition by scales and copper. The adopting father (technically the purchaser) would say: "I affirm that this son is mine according to Quiritary right, and he is purchased by me with this piece of copper and these copper scales." He would then strike the scales with the piece of copper, and give it to the seller (the natural father) as a symbol of the price.

If you are wondering what 'according to Quiritary right' means, it means according to Roman law; and a Roman citizen was called a Quirite. Therefore the adopting father would acquire the son from his natural father by the right of Roman law.

To emphasise how serious a step it was to buy a son out from under his natural father's patria potestas - the sale was carried out three times! Twice the natural father symbolically sold his son, and twice he bought him back. But the third time he sold his son, he did not buy him back again. Thus the natural father's power, his patria potestas over his son was regarded as being broken.

The Vindicatio

After the sale came the Vindicatio, which in Roman law was to present a legal case for the enforcement of the right of ownership. I believe it was named as such because, when successful, it gave the one presenting the case, vindication. In the matter of adoption, the adopting father went to a Roman magistrate and presented a legal case for the son - who had previously been sold and bought by him - to be transferred out from under his natural father's patria potestas and to come under his patria potestas. After presenting the legal documents of sale, the father was then asked to state if he wanted the one he had purchased to be his lawful son; and the son who was there to be adopted was asked to state if he wanted him to be his lawful father. That having been done, it was then down to the magistrate as a representative of the People to confirm, ratify and enforce the transaction on behalf of the People of the Roman Empire.

The adoption was then made complete and legal, and the adopted son came under the new father's absolute authority and control. From this point on the adopted son lost all rights linked to his old life and old family; and gained all the rights of a fully legitimate son in his new family. In the most literal sense, and in the most legally binding way, he got a new family and - *a new father*.

The consequences of this were.....

1) Legally the old life of the adopted son was completely wiped out. For instance if he had accumulated debts as the son of his natural father, now as the son of his adopted father, all his debts were legally cancelled. They were wiped out as though they had never been! The adopted son was now regarded as a new person entering into a new life, *which the past had nothing to do with!* In the eyes of the law, now that he had been adopted, he was literally and absolutely the son of the new father!

2) He became an heir to his new father's estate. Even if there were other sons who had been born of the father, who were real blood relations, he was a co-heir with them and those rights could not be taken away from him - by anyone! His inheritance was protected under a Roman law, called the Law of Adoptia.

3) Because he was legally adopted and the paperwork had been stamped with an official seal and registered with the magistrate's court, the law would not allow the father to disinherit him. Whereas, in contrast the father could disinherit his natural born son and the law would have nothing to say about it at all.

Chapter Four

The Ceremony

When the time came that was set by the father he would hold an official ceremony to place the son he had chosen in to the position of his son and heir. He could chose either a natural born son, or one who had been legally sold and bought by him. For the ceremony the father would assemble his whole household together, plus invited guests. When everyone was assembled the father would acknowledge that this was the son that he had chosen for adoption to sonship. From that time forward the assembled group knew that they were to treat this mature son, this *huios*, as the father's son and heir in all things. To confirm this new position the father gave the son a new name; and he placed a signet ring, containing his seal, on the son's finger. The new name and the seal was the confirmation of his status; and it was all that was needed to give the son credence in the eyes of everyone he would meet.

The Witnesses

To ensure there were no problems, among the invited guests at the adoption ceremony, were seven people who were asked to be official witnesses. This was so that when the father died, if there was a dispute about the right of the adopted son to inherit, one or more of the original seven witnesses could step forward and swear that the adoption was genuine and true. Thus the adopted person's right was guaranteed.

The Signet Ring

The signet ring, which contained the father's seal, was an outward sign of the legal transaction that had taken place. It was a guarantee of who they now were, and who was validating them as such. The word signet comes from the Latin words *sigillum*, which means seal, and *signum*, which means sign. A signet ring was so called because it contained a small seal, which represented someone's signature in picture form. These days with education most people can sign their own name with pen and ink; but before then those people who had any authority used a seal.

All seals, including those set into rings, were personal to their owners and enabled other people to recognise who they belonged to. In the case of letters, documents and scrolls, a seal was used to identify who the writer or the sender was. The way this worked was a candle would be lit and the wax was allowed to drip onto the paper or parchment. Then the sender would press their seal into the soft wax. The seal was engraved in reverse so that when it was pressed into hot wax it would show the design the right way round. Pressing the seal into the wax validated and sealed an agreement 'in the name of' the seal's owner. Then the document or letter would be rolled up or folded and 'sealed' with the wax, in order to make sure it couldn't be surreptitiously opened by another person before it reached its legitimate destination. The waxed seal would have to be broken in order to open and read the document and that would mean dire consequences for anyone other than the rightful recipient. The seal was a vital part in validating any document when making an agreement. Because it was only when the seal was broken by the rightful recipient that the agreement was completed and made legal.

A seal and wax was also used when something had been 'sealed' shut. Jesus' tomb is a clear example in scripture of something that was sealed shut. After Jesus had been crucified and His body had been laid in the tomb of Joseph of Arimathea, at the first opportunity the chief priests and Pharisees went to see Pilate. They were concerned that Jesus' disciples would steal His body away and claim that He had been raised from the dead. '"Take a guard," Pilate answered. "Go, make the tomb as secure as you know how." So they went and made the tomb secure by putting a seal on the stone and posting a guard.' (Matthew 27:65-66).

I doubt if Pilate gave the guards his own signet ring in order to seal the tomb. I would imagine it would have been a larger seal that was available to be used for official Roman business. My guess is that wax was poured on to either end of a piece of string or leather that had been fixed to the outer edge of the rocky tomb and across to the stone that had been placed over the opening. Then the seal would have been pressed into the wax on both ends, thus ensuring that no one could break the seal and steal the body. But it seems the angels weren't worried about the dire consequences that breaking an official Roman seal could bring!

Each seal that was made was unique and recognizable by all. In most of the cultures in biblical days the design would contain symbols depicting nature, animals, mythological figures and ancient gods. They were usually designed to display symbols of power and prestige, such as lions and griffins, thus giving much prestige to their owner.

Signet rings were very important in Roman culture because they were symbols of the authority granted to warriors and senior officials by their Roman emperors.

These rings would be engraved with symbols of their gods or they could represent a victorious battle scene they had taken part in. Often the face of the emperor, who granted the authority that the ring symbolised, would be engraved on it.

It was the expansion of the Roman Empire that helped to popularize signet rings among the peoples of the remotest countries of western Europe, including France and the UK. Just as with the Romans, local senior officials and important people wore signet rings signifying their authority and power. When the Roman Empire declined, the Byzantine Empire became established in the countries around the Mediterranean; and the signet rings they produced were heavily influenced by Christianity. Many of their signet rings and seals contained Christian symbols and Biblical teachings. But they weren't adverse to mixing Christian symbols with pagan ones too!

Legal documents need to be validated by signatures, whether that signature is written with pen and ink as it is now, or with the signature of a personal seal pressed into hot wax, as it was then. Having a seal's validation on it meant that the legal document or decree that had been issued could not be revoked or reversed. The nearest equivalent we have is when someone makes a will. Only another later will, signed by that same person, can supersede and invalidate the original will's contents. Otherwise it cannot be revoked or reversed.

'Ben Hur'

One of the best illustrations I have seen of this adoption ceremony is in the original film version of 'Ben Hur', which is subtitled 'A Tale of the Christ'. I haven't seen the updated version of the film, and although it may be illustrated in the same way, the version I'm talking about features Charlton Heston as the title character. The story centres around Judah Ben Hur, a man from a noble Jewish family who was arrested for what the Roman officials saw as an attempt on the life of the new Roman governor who had recently arrived in Jerusalem.

Although innocent, he is found guilty and his punishment meant he was taken to be a galley slave on a Roman battle ship. Ships in those days didn't have engines, they relied on a large number of slaves held below in the galley to row the ship to its destination. There was a man beating out a rhythm on a drum which indicated how fast the 200 galley slaves had to row. Each beat meant a stroke of the oar. The faster the beat the harder they would row and the quicker the ship moved.

The commander of the whole fleet, and the ship that Ben Hur was a galley slave in, was a high born Roman Consul called Quintas Arias. During a battle at sea, the ship that Judah Ben Hur was rowing in, was rammed by another ship. That act of ramming directly hit the galley where the slaves were; and they would have all died had not Ben Hur been the means of freeing them before the ship went down. As he emerged from the galley below to the deck above, Ben Hur saw the high born Roman Consul being swept overboard. To cut a long story short Judah Ben Hur saved the life of the Roman Consul and as a result was taken to Rome.

After riding in the Consul's chariot of honour in a victory parade. Ben Hur was given by Caesar to the Consul as his personal slave to do with as he pleased. The next scene shows us that the Consul has not only given Judah Ben Hur his freedom, but he has obviously taken him into his household, as a close family member. In fact more than that, because the scene is a big celebration, which is taking place in the Consul's lavish home.

To get the attention of all those gathered, the Consul claps his hands and asks for everyone's attention. He reminds those gathered there that his own son has tragically died; but goes on to say that this young man (pointing to Judah Ben Hur) has been more than a son to him since he arrived. Then he beckons Judah to come out and stand beside him. In front of all those gathered around he states that that Judah Ben Hur is to be his son and heir; and is now to be known by a new name - his name!

Here was a Jewish adult man, who was once a convicted criminal under sentence as a galley slave, being given the name of a prominent nobleman of Rome. In modern times he may have been named Quintas Arias Junior. But in those days, in a Roman household, he was named and known as Young Quintas Arias.

It's worth taking a look at the dialogue that took place in the film, as it is typical of what a father would have said at a Roman ceremony of adoption. Addressing those gathered around, Consul Arias tells them......

"The formalities of adoption have been completed. Young Arias is the legal bearer of my name and the heir to my property."

Consul Arias then turns and says..... "This ring of my ancestors would have gone to my son, so now it is yours.".

He takes the signet ring off his finger and puts it on the finger of Young Arias, who then replies......

"It's a strange destiny that brought me to a new life, a new home, a new father. It brought me here and it may take me away. But wherever I may be I shall always try to wear this ring as a son of Arias should - with gratitude and affection, and with honour."

There is more cheering and Consul Arias says....

"I present my son to you - Young Arias!"   And those assembled there as witnesses cheer once more.

From that point on wherever Young Quintas Arias (formerly Judah Ben Hur) goes, he only has to show the imprint of the seal made by his signet ring to those he meets, to prove who he now is. The proof of the seal from the signet ring that he wore had the immediate effect of him being given the honour and respect that was rightfully due to the son and heir of the Roman Consul Quintas Arias.

Interestingly, later in the film we see the commander of the Jerusalem garrison impressing the seal in his signet ring into a document. This time it wasn't an important document that was being sealed. The commander used his seal in order to confirm his wager on who would win the famous chariot race, that is a highlight of the film. The commander 'made his mark' and the wager was sealed and settled.

Chapter Five

Adoption in the Old Testament

This system of adoption to sonship was part of the tradition and culture of many countries, including Israel, thousands of years before the rise of the Roman Empire. The ceremony of adoption, if not the same legal procedure, was a known practice from very early times. Once we understand this we can see this practice referred to in the Old Testament.

A good example of this is Abraham and Sarah, or Abram and Sarai, as they were known for most of their adult lives. They lived mainly nomadic lives and Abraham was a very wealthy man, having much livestock, as well as silver and gold (Genesis 13:2). He also had very many servants, in fact he had enough men to wage a war against four kings! Those four kings had captured his nephew Lot from the city of Sodom, where Lot happened to be living when they attacked it. So Abram and the 318 trained men 'born in his household' went in pursuit of them (Genesis 14:14-24). Under Abram's command they thoroughly beat the kings, they freed Lot and restored his possessions to him. They also acquired the spoils but he refused to keep them, so that the king of Sodom couldn't say that he had made Abram rich. Abram was certainly rich enough before that battle, but all his wealth and his large household meant nothing when he considered the fact that he didn't have a son and heir to pass it all on to. Instead the only prospect he had with regards to an heir; the only choice he had regarding someone to take over the responsibility for his goods, his household and his and Sarai's welfare in old age - was for him to adopt as a son, his most trusted servant...

'When the word of the Lord came to Abram in a vision: Do not be afraid, Abram. I am your shield, your very great reward.
But Abram said, "Sovereign LORD, what can You give me since I remain childless and the one who will inherit my estate is Eliezer of Damascus?" (Genesis 15:1-2).

His choice of Eliezer would have been based on years of observation of the man's character and the assurance that everything that belonged to Abram would be taken care of in a way that he would have approved of. He must have been a man Abram could also rely on for his and Sarai's welfare in old age. But contemplating placing Eliezer, a servant, in the position of his son and heir, was obviously considered a poor substitute for the son that Abram and Sarai had always longed for.

The stages in the life of a Jewish male in both Old and New Testament times, were similar to those we have seen in the stages of those who lived in the Roman Empire; and to those in the other cultures around them. The main difference being that the first stage of life was marked in a totally different way than that of any other nation around. That first stage was marked by circumcision, which happened when a baby boy was only eight days old. Circumcision brought that baby boy into a covenant that was instituted by God Himself. It came about when He spoke with Abraham centuries before the Nation of Israel actually came into being (Genesis 17:9-14). The covenant was made between the Lord God and both Abraham and his descendants. But the covenant depended upon his male descendents being circumcised. Because it was circumcision, and not just being a descendent of Abraham, that set them apart as being in covenant with the Lord God.

Despite Abraham having many descendents, it was only those descended from his son Isaac and his grandson Jacob that carried on the covenant procedure of circumcising their male babies at eight days old. These descendents became known as the nation of Israel. Therefore when a baby Jewish boy was born, it was and is, vital for him to go through the ceremony of circumcision, so that he, like his ancestors, can enter into the same covenant that Abraham had. Circumcision marks him out, as young as he is, as being in covenant with the Lord God Almighty.

The second stage of the life of a Jewish male was, and is marked by his 'Bar Mitzvah', which means 'son accountable'. The Bar Mitzvah signified that the boy was now accountable to keep the Law and Commandments that had been given to Moses by the Lord God on Mount Sinai. It also meant he was now of an age to leave his mother's side and become an apprentice under his father in the family business.

The final stage in a Jewish male's life came when he was around the age of thirty. This important event was marked by yet another ceremony - the ceremony of adoption. The actual time the ceremony took place was the father's decision to make, when he thought the son was ready, when he considered his son was physically and mentally mature enough to take on important family responsibilities. It was then that the father would call the whole village together. The villagers were there to be a part of the celebration and to be witnesses to what he was about to do. When they were gathered the father would make a public declaration. He acknowledge that this son had now reached the age of maturity and he was pleased to declare that this son was now to be adopted as his son and heir. That declaration meant that from this day forward the son had full rights of authority and power over all that he owned.   As his father's heir and representative, the son had the right to carry out any business necessary on his behalf.   In essence he was saying that this son was to be treated with the same honour and respect, and in the same way - as if he was the father himself!

Not surprisingly it was at the age of thirty that a descendent of Aaron entered the priesthood and the Levites were allowed to enter the service of the Lord at the tent of meeting (Numbers 4:3).   Also it's no co-incidence that David was thirty years old when he was finally anointed king over Israel and Judah (2 Samuel 5:4); and that it was at the age of thirty that Joseph entered the service of Pharaoh, king of Egypt (Genesis 41:46).

For further confirmation of adoption to sonship being something that was a part of Old Testament culture and practice, we only need to look at Romans chapter nine. In this chapter Paul speaks of his anguish that the majority of the people of Israel are unaware of the amazing benefits of Christ's sacrifice for all men. He lists all the benefits they have already received under the Old Covenant, while desperately wanting them to understand and appropriate the benefits that could be theirs under the New Covenant. Paul writes...

'Theirs is the adoption to sonship; theirs the divine glory, the covenants, the receiving of the law, the temple worship and the promises. Theirs are the Patriarchs, and from them is traced the human ancestry of the Messiah, who is God over all, forever praised!' Romans 9:4-5

This passage in Romans tells us clearly that the nation of Israel was chosen by our Heavenly Father to receive the adoption to sonship. That Israel was adopted, placed in the position (*huiothesia*) of His son; and placed in the privileged position of being the Father's representative here on earth. The intention being that they would be a witness to the world to the character and goodness of the Lord God, the Father of all mankind. Witnesses to the power and the glory of their Heavenly Father the One True God.

Like an athlete is chosen, or placed in the position, to be a representative of his or her own country; whatever they do and achieve, they do and achiever it on behalf of their country. The athlete's glory becomes their country's glory; but conversely the athlete's defeat becomes their country's defeat. In that same way when Israel received adoption to sonship, when Israel was placed in the position of a son by our Heavenly Father, whatever they did or achieved, they did it or achieved it as a representative of their Father, the Lord God. Israel's glory became the Father's glory; but when Israel was defeated the true glory of the Father was marred and obscured to all the other nations around them.

The most memorable time that they fulfilled their position of being the Father's adopted son was when they were under the leadership of Joshua. All that they had done and achieved since they had left Egypt had been watched and carefully marked by the nations around them. But under Joshua they truly fulfilled their potential of bringing glory to the Father, as recorded in the statement that Rahab, the prostitute, made when she hid the two spies - 'I know that the LORD has given you this land and that a great fear of you has fallen on us, so that all who live in the country are melting in fear because of you.' She then lists some of their God given triumphs and goes on to say, "When we heard of it, our hearts melted in fear and everyone's courage failed because of you, for the LORD your God is God in heaven above and on the earth below." Her statement revealed how the nations were now viewing, not only the people of Israel but the One they represented - the LORD God of Israel.

However their triumphs achieved in the Name of the LORD God were spasmodic and over time dwindled away because of idol worship. It became evident that Israel was not fulfilling what was expected of an adopted son in regard to acting according to who their Father was. So it was time for the Son to come forth who would act as a true representative of the Father. A Representative that did 'run the race' and overcame all the obstacles and won the prize (Hebrews 12:1-2). Through complete obedience to His Father's will, Jesus achieved glory for His Father. He was the perfect Son. He truly displayed what it meant to be His Father's representative here on earth. What it meant to be, and act like, One who had received adoption as a Son and Heir of the Father. Not only that He made it possible for us to receive adoption as sons, and be heirs of the Father, too.

The Signet Ring in the Old Testament

'Then Pharaoh took his signet ring from his finger and put it upon Joseph's finger. He dressed him in robes of fine linen and put a gold chain around his neck.' Genesis 41:42

Joseph, having been wrongly imprisoned for many years, was finally released in order to interpret Pharaoh's dream. Joseph not only interpreted the dream he then proceeded to advise Pharaoh how to make provision for the seven lean years of famine that would follow the seven years of great abundance. Seeing the wisdom of God contained within this young man, Pharaoh decided to give Joseph the job of putting that advice into action. As well as dressing Joseph for the part and putting a chain of office around his neck, Pharaoh took off the signet ring he was wearing and put it on Joseph's finger

(Genesis 41:42). Without this signet ring, he may have looked the part, but Joseph would not have been able to implement the decisions he needed to make. Pharaoh's ring contained the royal seal; and the use of it authenticated and validated every decision Joseph made - just as if he was the Pharaoh himself. The result of this was the nation of Egypt was saved from starvation; and so were all the other nations around Egypt who came to buy grain. This included the embryonic nation of Israel that came from the descendants of Joseph's own family.

There is another great example of the legality and irrevocable power of the seal in the book of Esther. At first the legality and power worked against her and her people the Jews - but later it worked in their favour.

King Xerxes was persuaded by Haman, who was one of his closest advisors, that 'it was not in the king's best interest to tolerate' the Jews. So he gave Haman his signet ring in order to issue and validate a legal decree that ordered the people of the king's provinces 'to destroy, kill and annihilate the Jews' (Esther 3:8-13). But when Esther, who was the wife and queen of King Xerxes, discovered this, she risked her life in order to try and persuade her husband the king to annul the decree. The king is horrified when he realises the implication of what he has agreed to. Because in issuing a decree to annihilate the Jews, he had also put his wife Esther under a death sentence, as well as her uncle Mordecai who has already proved his worth by foiling a plot to kill the king. So King Xerxes has Haman arrested and put to death and appoints Mordecai to take his place.

'The king took off his signet ring, which he had reclaimed from Haman, and presented it to Mordecai.' Esther 8:2a

But there was nothing the king could do about the decree that had been sent out issuing orders to his people to annihilate the Jews. That was because the decree had been sealed with his royal signet ring; and therefore it couldn't be changed, altered or made invalid. The only way to deal with this awful situation, the only thing that could be done, was to write another decree and seal that with the king's signet ring.

"Now write another decree in the king's name on behalf of the Jews as seems best to you, and seal it with the king's signet ring - for no document written in the king's name and sealed with his ring can be revoked." Esther 8:8

Mordecai wrote in the name of King Xerzes, sealed the dispatches with the king's signet ring, and sent them by mounted couriers, who rode fast horses especially bred for the king. The kings' edict granted the Jews in every city the right to assemble and protect themselves. (Esther 8:10-11). That second decree didn't, in fact couldn't, overrule the original decree. But it gave the Jews the right to defend themselves when they were attacked. Plus it showed the people of his provinces that in issuing this second decree the king obviously didn't want the Jews destroyed now. This gave the new decree more weight and influence than the original one. The result was that the majority of the people held back from attacking the Jews and some even fought alongside them. This meant that the Jewish people were saved from the fate that their enemy had planned for them and were able to rid themselves of those who truly hated them.

The Seal, the Cord and the Staff

Not all seals were incorporated into signet rings. It was more practical for a man who worked in the fields all day, to carry his seal on a cord around his neck, as it was important to keep the seal on one's person at all times. That is because the seal not only signified the authority of that person, it validated and sealed that man's business transactions. Therefore to lose the seal would be very serious indeed. In chapter 38 of Genesis we read all about Jacob's fourth eldest son Judah; and how his heritage and lineage was preserved through a woman called Tamar. But before we look at Tamar we first need to understand a bit of cultural background in order to understand the significance of what happened.

In biblical times when a woman married she left her own family and became a member of her husband's family. This was what happened in all the cultures of the nations in the Middle East, not just in the Jewish culture. If the woman was childless when her husband died, she was then given in marriage to her husband's brother. The purpose being that she could conceive and give birth to a son by her brother-in-law. That son would then be considered the heir to her dead husband's family line; and he would be able to claim what would have been inherited by her dead husband (Deuteronomy 25:5-6).

We are told that Tamar was the wife of Judah's firstborn son Er. But he was so wicked that he was put to death by the Lord. They hadn't had any children so widowed Tamar was given to Onan, Judah's second son to be his wife. But Onan was also wicked. He took upon himself to make sure that Tamar didn't become pregnant and therefore didn't perpetuate his brother Er's family line. So the Lord put him to death also (Genesis 38:6-10). Now Judah had a third son who was called Shelah who he deemed wasn't old enough for marriage yet. So Judah told Tamar - "Live as a widow in your father's household until my son Shelah grows up." For he thought, "He may die too, just like his brothers." So Tamar went to live in her father's household.' (Genesis 38:11).

Tamar was supposed to go back to her father's household until Judah's third son, Shelah, grew up. But as the years went by and Shelah obviously grew up, it seems that Judah had no real intention of giving Tamar to Shelah for his wife. This despite it being a recognised obligation that he should have fulfilled. By his action, or should I say inaction, of not allowing her to be married to his third son, Judah was condemning Tamar to a life of loneliness and barrenness. Because as a widow of Judah's household Tamar could not marry someone else from outside of that household without Judah's permission. A permission Judah wasn't likely to give, as that would bring shame upon himself in the eyes of the community. So without any prospects of marriage Tamar would have stayed in a state of perpetual mourning. She would not only have to wear widow's garments for the rest of her life, she would have to remain childless in a culture that only honoured women through their ability to produce sons for their husbands.

But let's get back to what this has to do with the seal and its importance. After many years Judah's wife died and Judah was left a widower. Tamar, who was still living in her father's house as a childless widow, realised that he would be missing his 'marital comforts'. This gave her the opportunity she needed to rectify the wrong that had been done to her. So she secretly dresses as a prostitute and sits beside the road that she knows Judah will be travelling on, and waits for him to come along.

'Not realising that she was his daughter-in-law, he went over to her by the roadside and said, "Come now, let me sleep with you." "And what will you give me to sleep with you?" she asked. "I'll send you a goat from my flock," he said. "Will you give me something as a pledge until you send it?" she asked. "He said "What pledge should I give you?" "Your seal and its cord, and the staff in your hand." she answered. So he gave them to her and slept with her, and she became pregnant by him.' Genesis 38:16-18

It seemed to Judah that parting with his seal was just a temporary thing, a matter of convenience. He would soon have it back in his possession once he had sent the woman a goat. But he was totally unaware of who he had slept with and the importance of that seal to her.

Many people have read the story of Tamar in the Bible and judged her with regards to her deception and immorality. But I believe there is so much more to what she did than we realise. At face value it seems her desire to become pregnant and remove the stigma of being childless had caused her to lose her moral compass. But if all Tamar needed was to become pregnant by Judah, then why did she ask for his seal with its cord, and his staff as a pledge or a guarantee of payment? Surely, if she was just trying to get pregnant by appearing like a genuine prostitute and asking for payment, she could have just taken his word that he would send her a young goat. That would have been enough to make sure that he would carry out the necessary deed.

However, in asking for these important articles I believe that Tamar was protecting her reputation. She was making sure that everything was in place - before she undertook such a risky venture. After all she could be put to death once it became clear that she was pregnant outside of marriage. So she needed Judah to agree to give her his seal, cord and staff first; before she committed herself to such an outlandish action. Because having Judah's seal in her possession was as good as Judah putting his signature on a letter of affirmation that this was his child. It was as good as signing an affidavit or authenticating a legal document to that effect.

But she needed not only his seal but his staff too in order to claim the rights of his lineage for her child. That is because a man's staff had far more importance than we in our culture could ever understand. Let me explain: The word for staff in Hebrew is *matteh*, which not only means a staff or a rod; that same word *matteh* also means, a branch or a tribe. When God told Moses to hold up his staff over the Red Sea, the sea parted and the Israelites were able to cross over on dry land (Exodus 14:16). This was the same staff that God had told Moses to use to bring about the plagues in Egypt (Exodus chapters 7-10). The same staff that was a means of proving to Pharaoh that God had sent him. It was also the same staff that Moses had used when he had run away from Egypt as a proud young man. Because a man's staff wasn't just a stick he happened to have at that moment in time. A man's staff was personal to each man, because each significant event of the man's life, was carved or notched on it. A man's staff was like a journal, a record of his life to that point. It was a symbol of the experience that he had achieved in life so far; and the authority that he had gained.

Moses' staff had confirmed his identity, and that his authority was backed up by the power of the LORD God, both during the ten plagues and when the Red Sea was miraculously parted. Later, when a dispute arose among the leaders of Israel over his brother Aaron's right to be in authority over them as high priest. The Lord told Moses to put all the leader's staffs in the tent of meeting overnight. Putting their staffs in that tent was tantamount to putting their identities and their right to authority before the Lord overnight. Then in the morning it was found that only Aaron's staff 'had budded, blossomed and produced almonds' (Numbers 17:8). The fruitfulness that came from what seemed to be an ordinary piece of wood, was a declaration of the fruitfulness that was to come from Aaron's life. That staff, carved and notched with the account of Aaron's life, authenticated his authority and his position as high priest in the sight of God.

So when Tamar asked for Judah's staff, as well as his seal and cord, she was not just asking for a piece of wood, she was asking for the symbol of Judah's authority and his identity. Judah's staff was the testimony of who he was, which 'tribe' he belonged to, and the 'branch' of the family to which he belonged. Judah's staff was a validation of his personhood, as well as his position in the family and in the community. In asking for his staff was likè Tamar asking for the authority that validated and guaranteed his seal. In modern day terms the only thing we could equate with that is, it was like Judah was handing her his driving licence in order to validate his signature, which after all is what the seal represented.

'After three months Judah was told, "Your daughter-in-law Tamar is guilty of prostitution, and as a result is pregnant." Judah said, "Bring her out and have her burned to death." As she was being brought out, she sent a message to her father-in-law. "See if you recognise whose seal and cord and staff these are." Judah recognized them and said, "She is more righteous than I, since I wouldn't give her my son Shelah." And he did not sleep with her again.' (Genesis 38:24-26).

Of course Judah recognised his own seal, cord and staff, and he would have known exactly why she had asked for them. So he declared that Tamar was righteous, more righteous than he was, because he had refused to give her his son Shelah in marriage. Her righteousness came from the fact that, as his daughter-in-law, it was her right to bear children from Judah's family line. Having the proof that it was Judah's child she was carrying, meant that she and her unborn child would not be stoned to death. In the eyes of the community she was vindicated. Then when her time came, she gave birth to twin boys Perez and Zerah. A sign that in place of the barrenness and mourning, the LORD God had given Tamar a double portion!

Without Tamar being willing to risk everything to the point of losing her life; without her having the wisdom to obtain Judah's seal, cord and staff, Perez and Zerah would not have been conceived and born. In Matthew chapter one we find the account of Jesus' lineage; and it is there that we read that Perez was a direct ancestor of Jesus. Jesus was descended from Judah through his son Perez, who was the first of the twin boys to be born to Tamar. But not only is Judah and Perez listed in Jesus' ancestry, so is Tamar! She is there along with all the other important people in Jesus lineage - 'Judah the father of Perez and Zerah, whose mother was Tamar' (Matthew 1:3).

This seems to me as a vindication of the woman who so many have looked down on over the years. The writer of the gospel could so easily have left her name out of that illustrious list, but he didn't. I believe her being there is a confirmation and an honouring of her trust in God. We aren't told in scripture whether she was a Jew or a Gentile. But as Judah was not living alongside his father's family at the time all this was happening, she may very well have been a Gentile woman. Tamar is only one of three women to be mentioned in Jesus lineage by name. She is there listed with Rahab and Ruth as female ancestors, and both of these women were Gentiles. They were brought into the Jewish family and the Jewish faith through their trust in Israel's God.

Tamar may or may not have been a Gentile woman. But I believe that like both Rahab and Ruth, Tamar was mentioned in Jesus' lineage because she too was a woman of faith. Because in Romans chapter four we are told that the one who trusts in God, 'their faith is credited as righteousness' (Romans 4:5). The word 'credited' is an accounting term and is therefore reliable and accurate, not tentative and speculative. It shows that faith and righteousness are definitely interlinked. Tamar was declared as being righteous by Judah; and for Tamar to be one of only three women to be included, and recorded in Jesus' lineage, makes me think that it was her faith in God that brought about the birth of her twin sons.

NB: Throughout scripture there are instances of where the enemy tries to thwart the coming of the One who would 'crush his head'. When Haman tried to have all the Jews destroyed as recorded in the book of Esther is a prime example - no Jews, no Jesus. But I believe that what happened to Tamar and the wrong attitude towards her by Judah was also one of those instances - because the lineage of Christ was destined to come through Judah's line!

Without Tamar wisely asking for the seal, the cord and the staff; without her trusting God that she would conceive and give birth to a son - as she certainly couldn't have been able to go through that procedure again if she hadn't conceived, or had given birth to a daughter! Without her determination to make sure Judah fulfilled his obligation and rightful duty towards her, we are only left to wonder where the Messiah's linage would have come from. But her righteousness, her faith, made it possible for her descendant - the Messiah, the Lord Jesus Christ - to be born as the Lion of Judah.

Chapter Six

Adoption and the Stages of Jesus' Life

We don't read much about Jesus childhood. Matthew and Luke are the only two gospel writers who begin their account of Jesus' life with His birth. Whereas Mark and John both begin their gospels when Jesus is a grown man and is about to begin His ministry. My Bible dictionary says that Matthew probably drew a lot of his information about Jesus background from the apostle called James who, we are told in Galatians 1:19, was the Lord's brother. This makes sense when we see that Matthew's account is written mainly from Joseph's angle, and Joseph was James' father too. As we read through the first two chapters of Matthew's gospel we can certainly see that he records everything that a man would want to know, i.e. all the important facts and the tough decisions that had to be made.

Matthew begins with Joseph 's lineage, which show that Joseph was a descendant of king David through Solomon and the royal kings of Judah. Then he moves onto the tough decision of divorce and how Joseph went against his cultural upbringing by marrying Mary, his now pregnant betrothed bride. Matthew doesn't give any details about the actual birth of Jesus apart from where He was born and who the king was at the time. But he does tell us about the amazing arrival of the wise men and their valuable gifts. He explains that this visit of the wise men was the prelude to Mary & Joseph having to flee to Egypt with Jesus, because King Herod is about to kill all the baby boys under the age of two years old.

Matthew finishes his report on what happened after Jesus birth with one more tough decision. Having decided not to return to Judea because it was still dangerous, he decided they would go home to Nazareth. It was a tough decision because that was where Mary's reputation was not exactly great. But then neither was his, as he would be seen to be as the one who got Mary pregnant - or as the fool who didn't divorce her.

Luke's account of Jesus' birth and childhood however, in the first two chapters of his gospel, speaks about the people who were important in a different way in his description of the nativity story. He not only gives us the people's names but he also writes about their circumstances and how they were involved in Jesus' birth. He begins with the fact that Zechariah & Elizabeth were old and couldn't have children. He then records Zechariah's encounter with the angel in the temple, his response to the message from God, and the subsequent birth of John the Baptist. He contrasts Zechariah's response with Mary's, when she was visited by the angel Gabriel and told the good news of her being chosen to be the mother of Jesus, the Son of the Most High, on earth. He goes on to tell us what happened when Mary went to stay with Elizabeth when they were both pregnant.

Then he records all the details surrounding the actual birth of Jesus - why Mary & Joseph had to make the journey to Bethlehem; the heartbreak of there being no room for them in the Inn; and then he even tells us about the 'baby clothes' and the 'cot'! Luke continues by describing the amazing sight of the heavenly host of angels delivering their message to the shepherds, their terror at such a sight, and their hurrying off to Bethlehem to see the Infant.

The next piece of information that Luke gives us is that Jesus was named and circumcised at eight days old; and he follows it in the next verse by telling us about their going up to the Temple to present Jesus to the Lord. According to the Law 'Every firstborn male is to be consecrated to the Lord' (Luke 2:23); and Jesus was no exception. Mary and Joseph took the opportunity to do that when they went to Jerusalem to offer up the sacrifice required for Mary's purification. Although we read about this trip to Jerusalem in the very next verse, after the information about Jesus' circumcision on the eighth day, it would have been thirty three days after Jesus' birth that

Mary and Joseph would have gone to the temple in Jerusalem. That was the length of time a woman had to wait after she had given birth to a baby boy. She was purified to cleanse her from the bleeding that any woman experiences after the birth of a baby; and she was not allowed to go to the sanctuary before that purification rite had been performed. Interestingly Luke also records that they offered two birds as the sacrifice for her purification indicating that Mary & Joseph didn't have much money. He also tells us that it was there at the temple that they met first Simeon and then Anna. But Luke's gospel doesn't just tell us their names, he tells us the circumstances of why those two people were there, and what they said.

All of the above shows us that Luke's account of what happened surrounding Jesus' birth contains far more personal details than Matthew's account does. This has made many people, including me, wonder if Luke was in the privileged position of hearing all those details - from Mary herself? It's the details that raise this speculation, because, as most of us know - it's women that do details! As Luke himself says In Luke 2:19 - 'Mary treasured up all these things and pondered them in her heart.' As Mary was only a teenager when she gave birth to Jesus, and therefore would have only been about fifty years old when He died, many commentators believe that it was very possible that she was the source of Luke's account of the nativity and what followed.

The book of Acts, also written by Luke, tells us that Mary was there in the upper room with some of the other women, and Jesus' brothers when the Holy Spirit was poured out (Acts 1:14 & 2:1). So there would have been many years for Luke to have come alongside her and got the story correct. Plus it makes perfect sense when the only other account of Jesus birth is in Matthew's gospel, which seems to be written from Joseph's point of view. Matthew's record of all those facts and hard decisions plus the personal details found in Luke's account means that together - these two gospels make a perfect fit. They are like two halves of a puzzle that together, give us the full picture of what happened from the perspective of both Joseph and Mary; from both a man and a woman.

'On the eighth day, when it was time to circumcise the child, he was named Jesus, the name that the angel had given him before he was conceived.' Luke 2:21

Verse twenty one of Luke's gospel clearly tells us that Jesus was named and circumcised on the eighth day after He was born. It was the custom in most if not all countries not to name a child at the time of its birth, as so many babies died soon after. So the interval of a week was usual before naming them, which in the Jewish culture coincided with the time for male babies to be circumcised. Circumcision brought a new born baby boy into the covenant that had been established between the Lord God and Abraham's descendents. It was not to be taken lightly, because every covenant requires the shedding of blood; and circumcision was, and still is, a blood covenant. Circumcision is not a general covenant, although it is required of all Jewish males; it is a personal covenant made between the Lord God and the individual - 'This is My covenant which you shall keep, between Me and your descendants after you: Every male child among you shall be circumcised; and you shall be circumcised in the flesh of your foreskins, and it shall be a sign of the covenant between Me and you.... and My covenant shall be in your flesh for an everlasting covenant.' (Genesis 17:10-14). Jesus' circumcision established Him as a descendent of Abraham, who was in a personal covenant with His Heavenly Father here on earth.

NB: Knowing the love that our Father God has for all His children, I wondered about Jewish girls. How could they be brought into a personal covenant with Him? Then something occurred to me that I offer for your consideration here. It occurred to me that a girl would be brought into covenant with the Lord God as the result of her circumcised father taking that covenant into her mother, and making a covenantal union, which resulted in her being born. Then as a wife she would be brought into her husband's covenant when they were joined as one through their marital union. It would be a personal union between her and her husband that made them one, and that oneness would make it a very personal covenant that she would come into with her Lord God.

The next thing we learn about Jesus is when He was twelve years old...

'Every year Joseph and Mary went to Jerusalem for the Festival of Passover.

When he was twelve years old, they went up to the festival, according to the custom.

After the festival was over, while his parents were returning home, the boy Jesus stayed behind in Jerusalem, but they were unaware of it.

Thinking he was in their company, they travelled on for a day. Then they began looking for him among their relatives and friends.

When they did not find him, they went back to Jerusalem to look for him.

After three days they found him in the temple courts, sitting among the teachers, listening to them and asking them questions.

Everyone who heard him was amazed at his understanding and his answers.

When his parents saw Him, they were astonished. His mother said to Him, "Son, why have you treated us like this? Your father and I have been anxiously searching for you."

"Why were you searching for me?" he asked. "Didn't you know I had to be in my Father's house?"' Luke 2:41-49

Jesus had stayed behind in Jerusalem when His parents had begun their return journey home to Nazareth. A whole day had passed before Mary & Joseph had discovered that Jesus wasn't with the group they were travelling with. So they had to return to Jerusalem to search for Him; and they eventually found Him after three days! He was in the temple courts, sitting among the teachers of the Law, listening to them and asking them questions. As anxious loving parents they couldn't understand how Jesus could put them through such a traumatic few days and they told Him so. But Jesus seemed quite puzzled by their reaction.

I'm sure, like me, most of us have wondered why our sinless, loving Lord Jesus acted in this way and caused His loving parents so much anxiety. Why did He not tell His parents where He was going? Well it's easier for us to understand what was going on when we know that the word 'Son' that Mary used here is *teknon*. As we've seen previously this is not a word that is used when speaking to young children, it is used when speaking of a boy who is now considered of an age to make certain decisions for himself.   A boy who has come to the age of no longer being under his mother's tutorage and watchful eye. A boy who is now old enough to be taught by his father, and who is in training as an apprentice. This word 'Son' or *teknon* gives us a clue as to why Luke is telling us that Jesus was twelve years old when He and His family travelled to Jerusalem for this particular festival. Because this was probably the time when Jesus, just like any other Jewish boy around that age, was 'Bar Mitzvah'd. That being so, after the ceremony Jesus would have been considered a young man; a full-fledged member of the Jewish community with the responsibilities that came with it.

To further illustrate this point it's worth repeating here what can be found in my book 'The Jewish Wedding and the Bride of Christ'*.   When a journey was to be undertaken in those days people tended to travel in a group. This was for security reasons, in order to keep them safe from the thieves and robbers that lay in wait for any unsuspecting traveller. Apparently the women and children travelled together ahead of the men. At the end of the day they would stop and set up a temporary campsite and then get the evening meal ready. This meant that when the men arrived later they would find the camp set up, and their meal ready for them to eat. Therefore it's reasonable to suppose that Jesus travelled with His mother to Jerusalem with the women and children.

Then in Jerusalem if Jesus was 'Bar Mitzvah'd as His age seems to indicate, in his new status as a *teknon* Jesus would no longer have been expected to undertake the return journey home with the women and children. He would have been expected to travel back to Nazareth with the men; thus arriving at the camp after the women had set up the camp and prepared the evening meal. His new status would have made Mary think that Jesus was travelling behind the women and children. That He was travelling with Joseph and the men of the group, now that He was a *teknon*. Also it would be understandable for Joseph to think that Jesus had mistakenly gone ahead with Mary and the other women and children, just as He had done on the outward journey to Jerusalem when He was still considered a *paidion*. This being correct, it makes it very possible that it took them until the end of that day before they realised Jesus was not among their travelling group. Because it wasn't until the men arrived in camp that evening, that Mary realised that Jesus wasn't with Joseph; and it wasn't until the evening when Joseph arrived with the men, that Joseph realised that Jesus wasn't in the camp waiting for him with His mother Mary.

Understanding this makes much more sense of why Jesus was surprised that His parents were worried about Him. Jesus was no longer a child - a *paidion* when His parents came looking for Him. As a young man - a *teknon* He thought they would have realised that it was important for Him to be there in the temple courts listening to and asking questions of the tutors, the teachers of the Law. As a young man He was there to learn what would be required of Him when He would finally take His place in His heavenly Father's 'family business'. He was there sitting with the teachers learning all He could as His Father's apprentice.

The next and final stage of Jesus' life was when He reached the age of around thirty years old when He was a grown man, a *huois*. It was then that we read of what I believe was Jesus' Ceremony of Adoption. Jesus went to the Jordan River to be baptised in water by John the Baptist. Jesus had never given in to temptation and therefore He didn't need to repent or be cleansed from sin. The reason He was baptised, which He told John when questioned about it, was - 'to fulfill all righteousness' (Matthew 3:15). I believe this cleansing act was in preparation for His part as the Bridegroom, which you can also read about in my book*. But it was also because of what was about to happen when He came up out of the river.

'As soon as Jesus was baptised, He went up out of the water. At that moment heaven was opened, and He saw the Spirit of God descending like a dove and alighting on Him.
And a voice from heaven said, "This is My Son, whom I love; with Him I am well pleased."' Matthew 3:16-17

I believe that this declaration was not just the Father confirming that Jesus was His Son. But that, in accordance with tradition, the Father was conducting His own Ceremony of Adoption. A ceremony that took place in front of witnesses as was required; a ceremony that placed Jesus in the position of being His Son and Heir.

We can see the confirmation of this from scripture, in that from that moment on, Jesus left his old life and began his new life. Adoption by His Heavenly Father meant that He was no longer under the authority of His natural father, Joseph; and He was no longer going to continue as a carpenter in Joseph's business. From that day forward Jesus was committed to going about His heavenly Father's business with the power and authority of the Father's Son and Heir. That ceremony of adoption gave Jesus the right and authority to act on behalf of His heavenly Father - just as if He was the Father Himself. Something that Jesus had been preparing for since he was a young man, a *teknon* sitting in the Temple courts at the age of twelve years old, listening to the teachers. Just as He told Mary and Joseph when they asked what He was doing there....

'Jesus gave them this answer: "Why did you seek Me? Did you not know that I must be about My Father's business."' Luke 2:49 (NKJV)

'"Very truly I tell you, the Son can do nothing by himself; he can do only what he sees the Father doing, because whatever the Father does the Son also does."' John 5:19
'"I have a testimony weightier than that of John. For the works that the Father has given me to finish - the very works that I am doing - testify that the Father has sent me."' John 5:36

Through that Ceremony of Adoption, witnessed by the community, the Father had placed Jesus in the position of His Son and Heir. Thus meaning that the works He was about to do were a confirmation that He was going about His Father's business. That He had been sent by the Father and had the same power and authority that Father Himself had.

Chapter Seven

The Apostle Paul or is it Saul?

It was the apostle Paul who established many of the early churches that were situated in the Roman Empire; and it was Paul who wrote the letters, that were passed from church to church, about believers receiving adoption as sons. Therefore it's useful, and interesting, to look at who he was according to history, as well as according to scripture. Most of our information comes from the book of Acts. Acts was written by Luke, who also wrote one of the four gospels. Having written the story of Jesus up to his resurrection in the gospel of Luke, in Acts he takes up the story of what happened after Jesus was taken up into heaven.

Much of Acts is about what happened when Paul took the gospel to the Gentiles who lived in the Roman Empire at that time. As Luke accompanied Paul on those missionary trips he was a firsthand witness to most of what happened and therefore was in the perfect position to write it all down. Also as a physician, Luke would have been able to bind up the wounds that Paul received from the hands of the antagonists who rejected his gospel message!

Paul was born in Tarsus and was originally spoken of, and known as Saul of Tarsus. Tarsus is a historic city that is situated in south-central Turkey, which is approximately 20 km inland from the Mediterranean Sea. In Paul's time it was an important place for trade and commerce and this resulted in Tarsus, and all those areas around it, being invaded by many conquerors over its long history. It was General Pompey, the great Roman statesman and general that led the Roman army in conquering Tarsus in 67 BC, thus incorporating it into the Roman Empire. The year after this 'incorporation' the inhabitants of Tarsus received Roman citizenship. Therefore when Saul was born in Tarsus around 5 AD, he was born not just to Jewish parents, but also to Roman citizens.

Throughout scripture we are given a certain amount of information about Saul's early life. In his letter to the Philippians he writes of himself that he was - 'circumcised on the eighth day, of the people of Israel, of the tribe of Benjamin, a Hebrew of Hebrews....' (Philippians 3:5). As a Jewish boy under the direction of his father, Saul would have been trained and educated in the Hebrew language, with much Jewish influence. But living in Tarsus he would have had both Jewish and Greek friends and he would have learnt Greek alongside the Hebrew language as he grew up. Something that would be vital in the work of the Kingdom in later life.

In those days three things were expected of all Jewish fathers. The first was to have their sons circumcised when they were eight days old. The second was to teach them the law when they reached the age of thirteen. The third was to teach them a trade, which was vital for any Jewish male in order to have self respect in the community. In fact it was said that he who doesn't teach his son a trade, is teaching him to be a thief!

Saul was taught how to make and repair tents, which came in very useful in later life, especially when he went to Corinth. It was there that he was invited by Aquila and Priscilla to join them in preaching the gospel and in teaching those who had come to faith. Saul, known as Paul when among them, stayed with Aquila and Priscilla for about two years - 'and because he was a tentmaker as they were, he stayed and worked with them.' (Acts 18:3). The trade of tent making, learned as a boy, enabled him to pay his way as a missionary. It also meant he kept his self respect, while earning the respect of others, and enabled him to encourage others to do the same - 'You should mind your own business and work with your hands, just as we told you, so that your daily life may win the respect of outsiders and so that you will not be dependent on anybody. (1 Thessalonians 4:11b-12)

Around the age of fourteen or so, Saul would have been presented by his father as an adult at the city forum, where he would have been accepted as a citizen of Tarsus alongside all the other young men who were presented that day. But he, like the other young men, weren't just accepted as a citizen of Tarsus. Paul was also accepted as a citizen of Rome. Because the city of Tarsus was part of the Roman Empire. From that day on he would be known as Saul of Tarsus, a Roman citizen (Acts 23:27).

This rite of passage, leaving behind his childhood and being recognised as a young man, would have given him the right and ability to make certain decisions for himself. Something that would have been very important a short time later. Because when he was still a young man Saul was sent to Jerusalem to study the Law in order to become a Pharisee, thus follow in the family tradition - 'I am a Pharisee, descended from Pharisees' (Acts 23:6).

Saul's tutor in Jerusalem was the very well respected Rabbi Gamaliel. He was a first-century Jewish rabbi and a member of the Great Sanhedrin in Jerusalem. The word Sanhedrin in Hebrew means 'sitting together', from which comes the words 'assembly' or 'council'. The concept of the Sanhedrin goes back to the time of Moses. Moses became overwhelmed with the burden of leading the nation of Israel as they travelled in the wilderness. As he was God's anointed leader, he was the only one who was considered able to judge between their disputes. So he was told by God to take seventy men, who were respected elders among the people of Israel, to the tent of meeting - 'Then the LORD came down in the cloud and spoke with him, and he took some of the power that was upon him and put it on the seventy elders.' (Numbers 11:25). These seventy elders, plus Moses, became the primary pattern of leadership and decision making; and was the basis of what followed when the people of Israel became established in the promised land. In every city an assembly was appointed , which was made up of twenty-three men. The uneven number was needed so that decisions could be reached without deadlock. The assembled city councils were both judges on behalf of the people and teachers of the Law; and they had full authority over the people.

The Great Sanhedrin that met in Jerusalem, of which Rabbi Gamaliel was a member, followed more closely the original pattern that had been established under Moses by God. In that it was made up of seventy men, plus the high priest, thus making seventy-one being the required uneven number for decision making. They met in the Temple courts and they 'held court' every day apart from the Sabbath and on Feast days. They had great power to bring any Jewish person to court, from the highest in the land to the lowest, and to conduct their trial there. The Sanhedrin were the only ones who could decide any questions that related to Jewish law.

Saul's teacher, Rabbi Gamaliel was known as the rabbi 'who was honoured by all the people' (Acts 5:34). His wisdom was demonstrated when Peter and John were arrested and brought before the Sanhedrin after performing many signs and wonders among the people. The members of the Sanhedrin, jealous of what was going on, wanted to put them to death. But Gamaliel stood up and cautioned them to be careful in dealing with the followers of Jesus and wisely said - "In the present case I advise you: Leave these men alone! Let them go! For if their purpose or activity is of human origin, it will fail. But if it is from God, you will not be able to stop these men; you will only find yourselves fighting against God" (Acts 5:38-39). Thankfully Gamaliel's words were accepted and acted on by the council; and they let Peter and John go. But not before they had given them a warning not to teach in Jesus' name, followed by a flogging to make their point clear!

We don't know much about Gamaliel in the Christian church, but according to those who have looked into his life, he was a man of wisdom and great judgment. This honourable Jewish rabbi had a profound effect on the early church, and on the worldwide church that grew out from it. Because he not only saved the lives of Peter and John, who were eyewitnesses to the life of Jesus on earth, but as the tutor of Saul of Tarsus, who became known as Paul the apostle, Gamaliel has indirectly affected the church we have today.

Having spent many years 'at the feet' of Gamaliel, one of the best teachers in Jerusalem, Saul himself became an expert in the finer points of the Law. Now a Pharisee himself, the young Jewish Rabbi Saul became a witness to the stoning of Stephen. Stephen was a believer described as - a man full of faith and the Holy Spirit (Acts 6:5). Saul was not only a witness to Stephen's death, the coats of the stone throwers were laid at his feet. Thus implying that he was in agreement with what was happening and was happy to look after their belongings while they did the deed! (Acts 7:58). This stoning was followed by a great persecution of those who believed in Jesus and followed His teaching. So many of the believers fled Jerusalem and went to other towns and cities.

It was when Saul was travelling to Damascus with letters from the Sanhedrin in his possession, authorising him to arrest believers and bring them back for trial, that he met with the risen Jesus and he became a believer himself. Jesus appeared to him surrounded by an incredibly bright light from heaven. This encounter caused Saul to fall to the ground, because that light was no ordinary light, it was the glory of the Lord. When he eventually got up Saul found he could no longer see, he was blind. Therefore those who were with him, had to lead him into the city. There Saul spent three days in total darkness, during which he didn't eat or drink anything (Acts 9:3-9). I would assume that, as a believer now, those three days of darkness and fasting would have been accompanied by absolute repentance for how he had previously persecuted and maltreated all those who believed in Christ.

Ananias, a believer who lived in Damascus was sent to pray for Saul's sight to be restored; and for him to be filled with the Holy Spirit. Then Saul, having spent several days with the disciples in Damascus began to preach in the synagogue there. This turned out to be a dangerous thing for him to do and he ended up having to escape the city by being let down the city wall in a basket - at night! (Acts 9:10-25).

We are told in the letter to the Galatians that Saul then went to Arabia. Maybe It was some of Gamaliel's wisdom that had rubbed off on him; but alongside that I'm sure there was a specific directive from the Holy Spirit to go. Because, as he told readers in Galatia - 'my immediate response was not to consult any human being. I did not go up to Jerusalem to see those who were apostles before I was, but I went into Arabia.' (Galatians 1:16-17). Rather than listen to the opinions of men about what the gospel meant to them, Saul received revelation direct from the Holy Spirit on his own there in Arabia. I believe it's why Paul had such an impact on the fledgling church and beyond; and why his words and letters were kept and written down for posterity. Having been schooled in the Old Testament scriptures by Rabbi

Gamaliel, Paul's in depth knowledge of the Word was brought to life by the Spirit of God in Arabia.

After Arabia Paul returned to Damascus; and it was another three years before he eventually went back to Jerusalem, but only briefly, and he only saw Peter and James the Lord's brother on that visit (Galatians 1:18-19). It was fourteen years before he return again to Jerusalem (Galatians 2:1). Paul tried to join the disciples, 'but they were all afraid of him, not believing that he really was a disciple.' The disciples were afraid because Paul had been so actively involved in persecuting the believers in those days after Jesus had returned to His Father. He was only accepted when Barnabus vouched for him and his fearless preaching of the gospel. But it wasn't long before he was sent back to Tarsus for his own safety, when certain Hellenistic Jews plotted to kill him (Acts 9:27-30). Once he returned to Tarsus he began preaching to the Gentiles in all the surrounding regions. Regions which would then have been under the control of the Roman Empire.

Many people think Saul changed his name to Paul when he converted 'from Judaism to Christianity'. But that's not correct. Saul was born a Jew and he remained a Jew after he had met Jesus on that road to Damascus. That meeting, that revelation of who Jesus was, resulted in Saul, a Jew being 'born again', 'born from above'. The revelation he received was that Jesus truly was the

Messiah. The name Messiah means the 'Anointed One'. Whereas the original translators of the New Testament wrote His Name as Iesous Christos. Christians today know the Anointed One by the anglicised translation of His Name, which is Christ. Jesus Christ literally means Jesus the Anointed One. But to His Jewish disciples then, to Rabbi Saul, and to all those who are Jewish believers today, His Name is Yeshua HaMashiach.

The reason we read first of Saul in scripture and then later on as Paul, has a simple explanation. In the time of the New Testament, when it was mainly Jews who were spreading the gospel across the Gentile world, it was quite usual for Jews to be known by two names, one a Hebrew name and the other a Latin or Greek name. When Jesus appeared to Saul on that road to Damascus, He called him by his Hebrew name - "Saul, Saul, why do you persecute me?" Later when he was travelling around the Mediterranean, establishing churches and writing letters he used, and was known by, his Latin name of Paulus. In our Bibles today we read of him as Paul because that is the English translation of the Latin name Paulus.

Using the name Saul or Paulus, depended on who he was with, or who he was writing to. It was his way of making people feel at ease. It enabled people to relate to the man who was known as Paulus, when he was travelling around the Greek speaking world. Whereas the

Jewish people could far more easily relate to the man who was known as Saul when he was in Israel. As he put it - 'I have become all things to all people so that by all possible means I might save some.' (1 Corinthians 9:22b). Therefore using the name Paul instead of Saul had nothing to do with his spiritual new birth. It just depended on where he was or who he was writing to.

Paul was someone who knew the Old Testament through and through. The foundations that were built into his life by the knowledge of the law, the history and the prophets of the Old Testament were good and they were strong. However, the life that was built on those good foundations, was sadly perverted by legalism. A legalism that was learned from ambitious, religious men who were the leaders and members of the Sanhedrin at that time. As Saul, he never met Jesus while He was living on earth. But there is no doubt that he met the risen Lord Jesus in person on that road to Damascus. It was that meeting that demolished the 'legalistic building' that had been his life up till then. From that point on Saul's life was re-built on those good, strong foundations of the Old Testament and a new spiritual, Spirit filled building was erected. His life was re-built with a combination of a deep understanding of the scriptures coupled with the revelation of who Christ was. That new 'building' of his life was established in and through a relationship with the One who had inspired the writing of the Old Testament scriptures; and who in turn inspired

Paul to write a good part of what we call the New Testament today.

In Saul/Paul's words we have an amazing joining of the New Testament and the Old Testament in both the revelation of the Spirit and the enduring Word of God. It may be said that certain things Paul has written has puzzled some believers. But one day those puzzling passages will become clear and we will all understand the fullness of what he originally meant, before his words were transcribed from language to language over the years. As for the overwhelming majority of what he has written we can only admire the grasp Paul has on the message of salvation and life we can live in the power of the Spirit. And with a little knowledge of the culture of the time there is so much more that we can understand and enter in to.

Paul's teaching of receiving the adoption of sons is a great example of just such an amazing insight that has been obscured over the years; and like a hidden gem, this teaching deserves to be brought to the light once more.
Therefore let's now go to the passages of scripture that refer to the adoption of sons. Let us look at them in the light of all we've understood, about the ceremony and those things that were associated with it, so far. Things that Paul knew all about and wanted to impart to believers, when he wrote those passages down.

Chapter Eight

Adoption in the New Testament

'For He chose us in Him before the creation of the world to be holy and blameless in His sight. In love, He predestined us for adoption to sonship by Jesus Christ, in accordance with His pleasure and will -' Ephesians 1:4-5

In Roman, Jewish and most other cultures of that time, adoption was the most important thing that could happen to a man. So when Paul wrote in his letters about 'receiving the adoption as sons', all those who read them - *knew exactly what he meant!* Paul's original readers didn't read this statement as their being adopted like a child into the family of God. They read this statement as it was intended. That they were chosen to receive adoption, chosen to be placed in the position of being a son and heir of their Heavenly Father! This was incredible and of huge significance!

It must have given them a wonderful revelation of the fullness of what it truly meant to be a believer in Christ. That as a born again child of God they were not only a member of His family by new birth. They had also been chosen, before the creation of the world, to be the Father's son and heir by adoption. It's an amazing thing if we can grasp it like they did. That we have been brought into that privileged place through Jesus Christ, who took our sin upon Himself in the way that our Father had planned and predetermined. That our place in His family, and our adoption as His sons and heirs has been confirmed. That we have been sealed by, and with the Holy Spirit and our inheritance is guaranteed.

But hold on there's even more wonderful revelation to come. I'm quoting this from the New Kings James version of the Bible, as some of our more modern translations obscure what Paul and the original Greek translation was actually saying......

'For you are all sons of God through faith in Christ Jesus. For as many of you who were baptized into Christ have put on Christ. There is neither Jew nor Greek, there is neither slave nor free, there is neither male nor female; for you are all one in Christ Jesus. And if you are Christ's, then you are Abraham's seed, and heirs according to the promise.' Galatians 3:26-29

What Paul is telling them, and all the other churches where this letter would have been passed on to, is that there is no distinction regarding nationality, which is fair enough after all Paul is a Jew and they are Gentiles. However, he is also telling them that there is no distinction of class either. It doesn't matter whether they are the lowest of slaves or the highest born of free man. That might have taken a bit of getting used to, but it wasn't totally unknown for a servant or a slave to be adopted as a son. But to say that there is no distinction with regard to gender when it comes to being an heir of the promise - well that really was something for them to get their heads round!

That is because it was only men who could inherit in those days; and it was only men, whether slave or free, who could be adopted as sons and heirs! But that's what Paul was telling them, and us. As far as the adoption to sonship is concerned - "You are all sons!" In other words, any woman who believes that Jesus died to take the punishment for her sin in particular; any woman who has been born again from above by the Spirit of God - she has been adopted as a son and an heir! There is no distinction in His Kingdom between men and women. There is no distinction as to who inherits by adoption; no distinction as to who is a son and heir.

It's Personal!

I'll never forget the day when I 'saw' that I was a son; when I understood what was meant by adoption to sonship. I danced around my bedroom saying, "I'm a son, I'm a son". That may sound strange to you, but it was very significant for me. Three of my four grandparents had died before I was born. The only living grandparent I had on both sides of my family discriminated against me because I was a girl. She openly favoured my brother and our cousins who were all boys, and she blatantly refused to treat me equally, despite my parents best efforts in trying to make her. My Nan had three sons, three grandsons and me, the only girl to be born into her family. Therefore I grew up feeling that being a girl was a disadvantage.

When, as a born again believer many years later, I discovered that I was a son in God's kingdom I was overjoyed. I had never taken up any offence over the fact that certain scriptures referred to sons and not to daughters. From very early on I had understood that it was not in my Father's character to discriminate. So despite not knowing why it only mentioned sons and not daughters, I was happy to trust that He had allowed this to be written down for good a reason. Then when I saw the reason why it only mentioned sons with regard to adoption, when I saw what I have written down in this book, I was overjoyed. My heavenly Father considered me, and all His daughters, worthy to be His son and heir. I had received the same authority and inheritance as any other son in His Kingdom. It was clear that the scriptures weren't discriminating against women. The reason for saying sons and not sons and daughters, was there all the time. It was just the correct interpretation of what our 'receiving adoption to sonship' meant, that was missing. Our Father has been telling us this truth for millennia but I for one, just hadn't seen it.

This is why I said right at the beginning of this book, that us girls don't need to change any scriptures that refer to sonship, in order to make them fair to the fairer sex. As His sons, we are included! Every true believer, whatever their race, status or gender, everyone who has been 'born again', 'born from above', has also been adopted as their heavenly Father's son and heir.

Chapter Nine

Our New Patria Potestas

As we've seen, in Roman times the father was the patria potestas in his household with complete control and authority over his family and his household. But when his son or slave was bought for adoption as another man's son, he lost all control and authority over him. That son or slave came out from his patria potestas and under the patria potestas of the new father.

We can parallel this with the fact that we were once under the control and authority of our natural patria potestas. In other words, we were under the control of our sinful nature. A nature that was passed down from our parents and grandparents, right back to Adam. A nature that was subject to deception and misdirection from 'the father of lies' (John 8:44). That sinful nature was inherited by us all as descendants of Adam; and in another parallel, that sinful nature also made us all slaves.

Because Jesus said - 'Very truly I tell you, everyone who sins is a slave to sin.' (John 8:34).

The only way out was for a new patria potestas to be found. One who would be willing to pay the price to buy us out of slavery; and who would be willing to adopt us as his son and heir. That way our old patria potestas, our old sinful nature, would have no more authority over our lives. That new Patria Potestas was our Heavenly Father.

Our Sale Price

Our Heavenly Father was the One who took pity on us in our slavery. He was the One who saw something of worth in us and wanted to make us His sons and heirs by adoption. So He gave permission for His Son to leave His side and come to earth to pay that price on behalf of Him. Not counting the cost of what it meant for both of them. When asked, His Son didn't argue. He was willing to come. He paid a price for us that weighed far more in heaven's scales than the copper that was required for the 'purchase' of a son that was to be adopted in the Roman Empire. The price that was paid was the most valuable that could be found. In fact it was the only price that could obtain our freedom and secure our adoption to sonship.

'For you know that it was not with perishable things such as silver or gold that you were redeemed from the empty way of life handed down to you from your ancestors, but with the precious blood of Christ, a lamb without blemish or defect.' 1 Peter 1:18

NB: Often this 'purchase' of us by Christ's precious blood is described in scripture by the phrase He 'redeemed' us. This is because to redeem means to 'buy back'; 'to transfer'; 'to compensate'; also it means 'to release', 'to deliver', 'to rescue' and 'to save'.

Our Vindicatio

Our Vindicatio, the action for the enforcement of ownership, was able to take place because all the legal work had already been accomplished by Christ on the cross. Through His death He had already taken away all that stood between us, all that prevented us from having relationship with our Heavenly Father; and His precious blood was the price that was paid to buy us and to make us His own.   This made it possible for our Heavenly Father to make it known that He accepted us; and that He wanted to be our Father, our new Patria Potestas.

Then on the day we responded in our hearts, declaring that we did want Him to be our Father, it was the Holy Spirit, the 'Holy Magistrate' of God's Kingdom, that confirmed, ratified and enforced the transaction by bringing us to new birth. At that moment, as the angels in heaven rejoiced (Luke 15:10) - our adoption was sealed in the courts of heaven!

The consequences of this were....

Legally our old life was completely wiped out. From that point on we were regarded as a new person, a new creation who had entered into a new life. A new life - *which the past had nothing to do with!* 'Therefore, if anyone is in Christ, the new creation has come: The old has gone, the new has come.' (2 Corinthians 5:17).

Our debts were legally wiped out, just as if they had never existed - 'having cancelled the charge of our legal indebtedness, which stood against us and condemned us; he has taken it away, nailing it to the cross.' (Colossians 2:14). We came out from under the obligation to obey our old patria potestas, the old nature of sin and death. We were given free choice, just as Adam and Eve in the beginning had. That is to obey our new Father, our new Patria Potestas.

We became an heir of our Father and a co-heir with Christ. It's an inheritance that cannot be taken away from us - by anyone! Because we have been adopted and we have the seal of His ownership upon us.

'Now it is God who makes both us and you stand firm in Christ. He anointed us, set his seal of ownership on us, and put his Spirit in our hearts as a deposit, guaranteeing what is to come.' (2 Corinthians 1:21-22).

Our Ceremony

With all the legal requirements having been taken care of, what followed in Roman times was the public acknowledgement that this son had been adopted as the father's son and heir. As we read in a previous chapter, the father called together at least seven witnesses and held a joyful ceremony making his son's adoption official in everyone's eyes. If there was a ceremony in Roman times, it made me wonder - what was our ceremony? Jesus had fulfilled all the legal requirements to place us in the position of the Father's sons and heirs, so what was the official public ceremony that acknowledged that?

   Well I believe that official ceremony could very well be our believer's baptism. I say this because the verses in Galatians three that tell us that we are all sons and therefore heirs, are sandwiched around the words - 'For as many of you as were baptized into Christ have put on Christ.'

'But after faith has come, we are no longer under a tutor. For you are all sons of God through faith in Christ Jesus.

For as many of you as were baptized into Christ have put on Christ.

There is neither Jew nor Greek, there is neither slave not free, there is neither male nor female; for you are all one in Christ Jesus.

And if you are Christ's, then you are Abraham's seed, and heirs according to the promise.' Galatians 3:25-29

Baptism is a public declaration that we have died to our old life and have been resurrected to a new life in Christ. We go under the water as if we are being lowered into the grave because our old self is dead. Then immediately we come up out of the water in demonstration of being resurrected into our new life in Christ. Baptism confirms that we are now a new creature; and we have a new Patria Potestas. We are no longer under the old patria potestas of our sinful nature, we are no longer obligated to follow its dictates; and the debts from our old life have been wiped out - as though they had never been.

For me it was not an easy decision to be baptised. Don't get me wrong, I really wanted to be baptised, but at the time I had an unbelieving husband and I had to get the whole church praying that he wouldn't object when I approached him on the subject. I'm pleased to say that prayer worked and when I told my husband that I wanted to be baptised he said I could - "But don't expect me to be there to watch you!" Well that was the first hurdle overcome. So I then asked the church to pray he would change his mind - which he did, on the night before my baptism! I could tell you so much more about what happened and how he came to change his mind, but you can read that in my book, 'How to Pray when he Doesn't Believe'.

That Sunday evening when I was baptised, as I came up out of the water, I was acutely aware of a sense of the Father's pleasure. On reflection, I realise it must have been how Jesus felt when He heard His Father say, - "This is my beloved son, with whom I am well pleased!" (Matthew 3:17), when He came up out of the Jordan River after being baptised by John the Baptist. I didn't hear any audible words myself, but I was filled with His peace, love, and joy - fit to bursting! I knew His pleasure wasn't just because I had overcome my personal hurdle and been obedient to His word to be baptised. Because all the other people who were baptised that evening were full of joy, as they too sensed the Father's pleasure.

Going back to the illustration of adoption to sonship in the film 'Ben Hur', I am reminded of the look of pleasure and pride on the face of the Roman Consul Quintas Arias when he was making the public declaration that Ben Hur was now his legally adopted son. I have witnessed many baptisms over the years, including my own husband's....; and I have seen their joy and know that they too have experienced the Father's pleasure, as they have come up out of the water. This is what made me wonder, 'Could baptism be our Ceremony of Adoption?' . My conclusion is - 'I believe it could be!'.

Our Witnesses

Our witnesses are those friends and family who were there at our baptism. Plus we are told in Hebrews 12:1 that there is a 'great cloud of witnesses' that surround us. But the most important witness to our new life in Christ is the Holy Spirit. Because it is the Holy Spirit who is the guarantee of our inheritance.

'But the Holy Spirit also witnesses to us...... ' Hebrews 10:15a (NKJV)

'When you believed, you were marked in him with a seal, the promised Holy Spirit, who is the deposit guaranteeing our inheritance until the redemption of those who are God's possession to the praise of his glory.' Ephesians 1:14

The Holy Spirit was the means of bringing us to new birth and He is the guarantee of our inheritance as a son and heir of our Father. He will step forward as our witness should anyone dispute our right to inherit. He will confirm that our adoption to sonship is genuine and true; and He does that with His seal - as the next section will reveal.

Our Signet Ring

In John's gospel we read of the miracle of feeding the five thousand with five loaves and three fish. The next day, after this amazing feast the people went looking for Jesus hoping to get more free food. So Jesus says to them - "Do not work for the food that spoils, but for the food that endures to eternal life, which the Son of Man will give you. For on him God the Father has placed his seal of approval." (John 6:27). The words 'of approval' aren't there in the original Greek; and they are not given in other versions of the Bible such as the New Kings James Version (NKJV) and the New American Standard Bible (NASB). The original just says - "For on him God the Father has placed his seal."

This makes things a whole lot more relevant in the light of what we now know. Jesus wasn't just saying that He had His Father's approval. Jesus was saying far more than that. He was saying that His heavenly Father had bestowed His seal upon Himself, as His chosen Son. That the Father had authorised Jesus to go about His - the Father's - business as if Jesus were the Father Himself. Just as a Roman father would bestow the signet ring containing his seal upon the son he had chosen for adoption to sonship. The Father had bestowed His signet ring containing His seal on His Son Jesus. That signet ring was the Holy Spirit, let me explain....

The disciples had been born again when the breath of life was breathed on them by Jesus after His resurrection - 'And with that he breathed on them and said, "Receive the Holy Spirit. If you forgive anyone's sins, their sins are forgiven; if you do not forgive them, they are not forgiven." (John 20:22-23). Then on the day of Pentecost these same disciples were endued with power as the Holy Spirit came upon them and filled them - 'All of them were filled with the Holy Spirit and began to speak in other tongues as the Spirit enabled them.' (Acts 2:4).

Some days later when Peter and John went up to the temple they saw a man who had been lame from birth asking for money. They either didn't have any money to give him or they didn't see the need to give him any money. Because they knew what Jesus would do in that situation. Therefore, rather than give the lame man money, they went about their Father's business and gave him healing instead. They said, "... in the name of Jesus Christ of Nazareth, walk." (Acts 3:6). The man was healed, which was a visible confirmation that the Holy Spirit was working though them. But it was also a visible confirmation that they too had been given the Father's signet ring, the seal of the Holy Spirit. Because His power impressed upon them, filling their lives, gave them the authority to go about their Father's business.

Ephesians 1:13b 'When you believed you were marked in him with a seal, the promised Holy Spirit.'

The Apostle Paul wrote to the Ephesians about their being sealed with the Holy Spirit, knowing that the letter would be passed to the other early churches that were situated in the Roman Empire. As he wrote he would have been aware that they would understand what he was saying about being sealed, as well as their receiving adoption to sonship.

'Now it is God who makes both us and you stand firm in Christ. He anointed us, set his seal of ownership on us, and put his Spirit in our hearts as a deposit, guaranteeing what is to come.' 2 Corinthians 1:21-22.

It is only modern day believers that aren't fully aware of what it means to be marked as being 'in Him' - with a seal. But once we understand, it's an amazing thing to know that we were 'sealed' with the Holy Spirit of promise. That we have had the Holy Spirit pressed into our lives - just as a seal is pressed into hot wax. We have been marked out as belonging *to Him*; and as being sent *from Him*. Subjectively it is difficult to see that in ourselves. But often other people will become aware that there is something different about those who are His. Something different about those who have been born again, born from above. We are not usually aware that they are picking this up. But just very occasionally someone will say, on finding out that we have faith in Christ, that they sensed there was something different about us. When someone becomes a Christian through the friendship of believers they quite often say this. They don't always know different. Also when meeting someone for the first time we can often recognise His seal on their what they are discerning, but it is the seal that He has impressed upon our lives that makes us life. There is a knowing deep down that they belong to Him, in the same way that we do.

Our New Robe

In the Roman Empire, when a child reached the age when his father presented him to the city forum as a citizen, he was given a new robe. The toga he had been wearing as a young child, as a *paedion*, which was called the toga praetexta, was exchanged for the toga virilis. That new robe declared to all he met that he was no longer a boy. He was now a citizen of the Empire with rights and responsibilities to make decisions on behalf of, and for the common good of the residents of their city. It also meant he was now able to make certain decisions about his own life instead of being under the constant supervision of a guardian.

When we are made citizens of the kingdom of God we are also given a robe to indicate our new status. It's a robe that declares we are now citizens of heaven, and citizen of God's kingdom here on earth. It means that we have been given rights and responsibilities to make decisions on behalf of, and for the common good of, all mankind.

The new robe, given to us by our Father - and paid for by our Saviour - is a robe of righteousness. It's a robe that we aren't given at a certain age; and it's not a robe that we can earn by merit, by doing good or even by being good. Because as the prophet Isaiah tells us - '... all our righteous acts are like filthy rags...' (Isaiah 64:6a). It is a robe that can only be bestowed upon someone at their new birth, on the day of their salvation. It is a precious and significant robe; a robe that covers us completely and encompasses us all around; and it's the robe that the Father sees when He looks at us. It's not easy for us to understand but when the Father looks at us He doesn't see our shortcomings, He sees that robe of Jesus' righteousness upon us, and we are accepted as His own - 'For he has clothed me with garments of salvation and arrayed me in a robe of His righteousness...' (Isaiah 61:10).

The picture language of being given a robe means so much more when we realise that in Biblical times a robe or cloak wasn't just a garment to wear. It had visual significance too, and not just for Roman citizens. Let me explain...

In the gospel of Mark (Mark 10:46-52) we read of a blind man called Bartimaeus, who was sitting by the roadside begging. When he heard that Jesus of Nazareth was passing by he began to shout, "Jesus, Son of David, have mercy on me!" Despite being told to be quiet, he shouted all the louder, which had the desired effect and Jesus stopped. Jesus then told the people to call him - 'So they called to the blind man, "Cheer up! On your feet! He's calling you." Throwing his cloak aside, he jumped to his feet and came to Jesus.' (Mark 10:46-50).

The very first thing this blind beggar did, even before he jumped up, was to throw off his cloak. This was incredibly significant. In throwing his cloak aside, Bartimaeus was making a declaration of faith. Because in those days a blind person didn't have a white stick to indicate their lack of sight, like they do now. Instead a blind person wore a particular cloak that told everyone around them that they were blind. By throwing that cloak aside Bartimaeus was demonstrating the faith he had in Jesus to heal him. He was disassociating himself with blindness - in the expectation that Jesus would give him the ability to see.

Without that full expectation of faith Bartimaeus might have taken the cloak off, but he would certainly have held

on to it. That was because there was a large crowd with
Jesus as He left the city; plus there were all those crowded
around him on the roadside. It would have made more
sense for him to have held on to that cloak - just in case!
Instead blind Bartimaeus demonstrated an amazing act of
faith in just throwing off that cloak knowing he would
probably not be able to find it again. It was such an act of
faith that Jesus didn't even have to lay hands on
Bartimaeus in order for him to receive his sight. He just
asked him what he wanted.   Bartimaeus replied by
saying, "Rabbi, I want to see." "Go", said Jesus, "your faith
has healed you." Immediately he received his sight and
followed Jesus along the road.' (Mark 10:51-52). Maybe,
as I have done, you have questioned why Jesus needed to
ask Bartimaeus what he wanted. Wasn't it obvious? Well
no, it wasn't as obvious as we would think.   Because
Bartimaeus had thrown off the very item of clothing that
indicated he was a blind man without sight - before he
reached Jesus. He'd thrown away his cloak!

 A couple of chapters later in Mark chapter 12 another
kind of robe or cloak is commented on by Jesus, when
referring to the hypocrisy of the religious leaders   -
"Watch out for teachers of the law. They like to walk
around in flowing robes and be greeted with respect in
the marketplaces, and have the most important seats in
the synagogues and the places of honor at banquets.
They devour widows' houses and for a show make
lengthy prayers.   These men will be punished most

severely." (Mark 12:38). Religious leaders also wore significant robes, which indicated their status in life. This time it wasn't the cloak of blindness (although Jesus, if asked, may very well have said it was!) it was a long flowing robe. It is described as a loose outer garment for men extending to the feet, worn by kings, priests, and persons of rank. Wearing this long flowing robe distinguished the teachers of the law from other people. It meant that wherever they went, everyone knew who they were - and how important they were! An importance that meant nothing, as Jesus so rightly indicated, if the actions of the robe wearer said something totally different about them! Interestingly the word used for robe here, which is *stolé*, is the same word we read of in Revelation 6:11 that is given to those who have been killed for their faith - a robe worn by kings, priests and persons of rank.

There are many robes and cloaks given or worn in the Old Testament that had significance. The most obvious one is in Genesis 37 where we read that Jacob made an ornate robe for his son Joseph because he loved him more than any of his other sons. This special robe set Joseph apart from his brothers; giving him the distinction of being the favourite son of Jacob (Genesis 37:3). Apparently a garment like this, which extended to the wrists and to the ankles, was the type of garment that was worn by boys and girls of a nobler rank than those around them. No wonder Joseph's brothers were extremely jealous of him and it didn't help when he told them of the dreams that he had had where the brothers were bowing down to him. That robe may have been very special and ornate; and it may have been an honour for Joseph to have been given it. But that robe sure didn't make his life an easy one.

It's interesting how special robes can stir up trouble with those who are close to the wearers! If people who don't have a robe of righteousness, who don't know Jesus as their Saviour, are subconsciously aware that you are wearing a robe of righteousness - don't be surprised if life doesn't always run smoothly! In fact if they are closely related and living under the same roof as you, they may make your life as uncomfortable as is possible. This was something I learned very soon after I'd been given my new robe. [If you want to read about my experiences in that situation, you can find all the details in my book 'How to Pray when he Doesn't Believe']

Another robe that stirred up trouble between brothers was the one spoken about in Luke 15 when Jesus told the story of, what we call, the prodigal son. When the prodigal son returned, his father called for 'the best robe' to be brought and put upon his son. In doing so he covered both his son's ragged clothes - and all his misdemeanors. But there's more to this than just clothing him. The word 'best' means first in time or place; or first in rank, influence and honour. Plus the word used for robe here is the same word we read above, it is *stolé* . We know this son was not the first in time, i.e. he wasn't born first; because we read of his older brother later on in the story. Therefore by the father putting the best robe, the *stolé*, on his younger, wayward son and not just giving him a clean robe to wear, he was definitely elevating him to a place of honour and restoring him to his place in the family and the household. Plus, by this action he was declaring to the neighbours, who would have gathered at the scene, that even though his son had wasted his inheritance in living foolishly, even though he had dishonoured his father, he was reinstating his younger son to the position of a son and heir.

It's worth noting that the actions of the father towards his son were more important than meets the modern eye. Of course this was just a story, a parable that Jesus told. But you can be sure that the original hearers of this story would have got the point Jesus was trying to make in far more detail than we can. Over the years the significance of the story has been unfolded as teachers have waited on God and have found out what different things mean. But Jesus' hearers would have known what He was saying in detail, because they lived in that Middle Eastern culture; and they knew about the customs and the covenant that was part of that story then. As I don't want to digress too far from the robe right now, the covenant referred to will have wait for another book.... But suffice it to say for now, that the fact that his younger brother had been given 'the best robe' when he arrived back home, would have rubbed even more salt into his elder brother's wound.

To finish this section, let's look at the woman who was subject to constant hemorrhaging for twelve years and the doctors could do nothing for her. Her story is so good, and is such a great example of faith, that it was written down in three of the four gospels, Matthew, Mark and Luke. But for our purposes let's look at it in Mark 5:24-34. Jesus was being followed by a large crowd and was almost crushed by the number of people around Him. As part of the large crowd, this dear lady managed to come right up behind Him and she touched His cloak. Immediately she was healed and the hemorrhaging stopped. Just as immediately Jesus knew that power had gone out from Him, and after asking who had touched Him, He discovered that it was her that had 'obtained' that power. Women were not allowed to touch men in those days without bad connotations. But Jesus commended the woman for her faith and said, "Go in peace and be freed from your suffering." (Mark 5:34).

It had taken all the courage that lady could muster to touch Him, thinking that He wouldn't notice with all the jostling that was going on. But Jesus knew the touch of faith filled hope. A hope that is described in Hebrews 11:1 - 'Now faith is the confidence in what we hope for and assurance about what we need.' It was her faith filled hope that drew the healing she needed, from Him.

During His time on earth Jesus didn't wear a special cloak, a noble cloak or a 'best robe'. He just wore an ordinary, everyday cloak. But when this lady touched His everyday cloak, she was by faith, actually touching - His robe of righteousness.

Our New Name

Just as Judah Ben Hur was given a new name at the moment his adoption to sonship was made official, i.e. 'Young Arias'. Believers in Christ are known throughout the world by a name that we didn't have before we were chosen for adoption. Unfortunately this name has become a generic term, and has been applied in a non biblical way to most people who live in European countries. I'm talking about the name Christian. Most of the countries in Europe were once known as Christian countries, because Christianity was the dominant religion. Whereas other countries that were beyond Europe were predominantly Muslim, Buddhist, Hindu, etc.

These days many European countries are multi cultural and multi faith. Therefore the term 'a Christian country' is not really applicable now. Many may still claim that title for their country and for themselves, because it's where they were physically born. But it is only those who have been 'born again', 'born from above' that can truly lay claim to that name. As someone once said, "If you were born in a garage, it wouldn't make you a car!"

The name Christian was first given to born again believers that lived in Antioch - 'And the disciples were first called Christians in Antioch.' (Acts 11:26b). In a previous chapter we saw that the English name Christ comes from the Greek word *christos*, which means 'anointed'; and Jesus is called The Christ, because Jesus is 'The Anointed One'. Starting at Antioch, and then moving out into in all the lands where the gospel was preached, Jesus followers were given the name Christian because they demonstrated that they too were 'anointed ones'. They were viewed as being 'Christ...ians'. Or in the terminology of the Ben Hur story, we could say that they were viewed as being a 'Young Christ's.

The use of the name Christian in a generic way began after more than two centuries of persecution of believers in Christ throughout the Roman Empire. A persecution that continued under a succession of Roman Emperors. That is until Emperor Constantine the Great came to power. As one report says, he looked up to the sun before the battle of Milvian Bridge and saw a cross of light above it, and with it the words - 'In this sign, conquer!'. So he commanded his troops to adorn their shields with a symbol made up of the first two Greek letters of the word Christ. He won the battle and from that point on he became the patron of the Christian faith.

He supported the Church financially, he promoted Christians to high-ranking offices, he returned confiscated property and he endowed the church with land and wealth. Then when he built a new city, which he named Constantinople, he required all those who had not converted to Christianity to pay for it! Thus anyone who wanted to hold onto their wealth, and keep in favour with the Emperor, 'became a Christian'; and the nations of Europe that flourished under his control became known as Christian nations.

Because the name Christian was 'high jacked' and applied to 'convenience believers' under Constantine, and to all those who 'happened to live in Europe', the title Christian has for most people become a generic term. In fact some of the actions that have taken place in the name of Christianity have totally misrepresented what Jesus Himself taught; and certainly not what true 'little Christ's would do. One example being the crusades where 'Christians' from Europe went forth to liberate the Holy Land in the name of Christ. These crusades resulted in the death of many innocent people, just because they were called Moslems or Jews.

Therefore those who live in the Middle East, and in what we might call 'difficult' countries, when they truly accept Christ as their Saviour and Lord they call themselves Believers instead. That is because to use the name or title Christian would not only cause that person great problems, it would invite active persecution for themselves and their families. Using the name or title Christian would convey the message that they have abandoned their culture and upbringing in order to take up another religion, the religion of Europe. Whereas calling themselves Believers conveys the correct message that - whatever their background - they have accepted Christ as their Saviour and they now have a personal relationship with Him.

For now all those who believe in Christ have either taken the name Christian or Believer. But one day according to the book of Revelation, they will be given a new name that is known only to them - 'To the one who is victorious, I will give some of the hidden manna. I will also give that person a white stone with a new name written on it, known only to the one who receives it.' (Revelation 2:17). This is a name which is to be revealed at the end of time and it will be written on a white stone. There are varying interpretations of what is signified by the white stone in scripture and all seem valid according to the information that I have come across. Here are a few examples....

If someone was brought to trial it was the custom in both Greek and Roman courts for a vote to take place using black and white stones. A black stone was cast indicating the accused was guilty, whereas a white stone was cast to indicate innocence. If the white stones outnumbered the black stones, then the accused was set free. If found not guilty, it was standard practice for the one who was acquitted to be given a white stone as proof of the verdict. This white stone was called the pebble of acquittal. As believers, we have been acquitted of the charges brought against us by the accuser of the brethren. The blood of Jesus shed for our sins provides us with that 'not guilty' verdict. It could be said that when we repent of our sin and receive His forgiveness, according to the custom of those former days, we have been given a pebble of acquittal.

A white stone was also used when casting lots in Greek elections. This eliminated the difference between the literate and the illiterate, as when someone who can't write has to 'make his mark' by putting a cross on a ballot paper. In Greek elections those who were eligible would be given a white stone and a black stone. They used them according to which candidates they wanted to be elected or rejected. So it could be said that we used our white stone in His favour when we elected Jesus to be our Saviour.

There are other meanings that are linked to being given a white stone, which are also just as applicable. One is connected to hospitality. A host would give a special guest a white stone, which had a name or a message written on it. That name or message was for the guest alone and it was not revealed to, and therefore not known by, anyone else.

A white stone was used to mark good days or festival days whereas bad days, days of disaster and calamity, were marked by a black stone. For us it will certainly be a good day, in fact it will be a wonderful day, when Jesus returns! A white stone was also used as an admission ticket to public festivals; and that Revelation white stone could be described as an admission ticket to the greatest festival of all!

Most of us know that at the original Olympic games held in Greece the victorious winners were given a wreath or crown made out of laurel leaves. But did you know that they were also given a white stone, which had the winner's name written upon it, as well as the value of the prize that they had won.

In the second letter of Timothy we read - 'Now there is in store for me the crown of righteousness, which the Lord, the righteous Judge, will award to me on that day - and not only to me, but also to all who have longed for his appearing.' (2 Timothy 4:8). In this life we have been given the name of Christian or Believer. But one day, according to these scriptures in 2 Timothy and Revelation, His victorious ones can look forward to being given both a wreath or a crown, and a white stone with our new name on it.

Chapter Ten

Adoption and the New Covenant

'But before faith came, we were kept under guard by the law, kept for the faith which would afterward be revealed.

Therefore the law was our tutor *to bring us* to Christ, that we might be justified by faith.

But after faith has come, we are no longer under a tutor. For you are all sons of God through faith in Christ Jesus.....

Now I say that the heir, as long as he is a child, does not differ at all from a slave, though he is master of all, but is under guardians and stewards until the time appointed by the father.

Even so we, when we were children were in bondage under the elements of the world.

But when the fullness of the time had come, God sent forth His Son, born of a woman, born under the law, to redeem those who were under the law, that we might receive the adoption as sons.

And because you are sons, God has sent forth the Spirit of His Son into your hearts, crying out, "*Abba*, Father!" Therefore you are no longer a slave, but a son, and if a son, then an heir of God through Christ.' Galatians 3:23-26 & 4:1-7 (NKJV)

It's easier to see what Paul was saying here when we have some understanding of adoption, sonship and inheritance. In childhood, a young boy was no different than a slave because he was constantly under the supervision and guardianship of a *paidagogos*. The *paidagogos* oversaw every detail of the boy's life and behaviour and he was authorised to use discipline, chastisement and instruction to make sure that boy acted in accord with what his father would expect from him. Paul, in this letter is likening the law to a *paidagogos,* or tutor, because in Old Testament times the Law was put in place to train up and educate God's people.

The Law, which was given by God to His chosen people via Moses, is also known as the Book of the Law. This was not just the Ten Commandments that Moses received on Mount Sinai. What constituted the Law was also made up of many practical laws about everyday living, attitudes, morals, behaviour, what is acceptable and what is not. It also contained instructions about food, health and hygiene.

When we read the words 'Book of the Law' or the 'Law'
in the Old Testament, the words are distinguished by
being capitalised, just as any name or title of God is
capitalised. That is because the Law was given to God's
people to be God's representative here on earth. God
could not come near to them in person, because the
people He had chosen for Himself, like the rest of
mankind, were sinful; and as a holy God He could not
tolerate sin in His presence. Therefore He gave them the
Law as His representative so that they would know what
they needed to do in order to remain in right relationship
to Him; and to live a good and peaceful life with each
other.

Through the Law God's people were instructed, guided
and disciplined. The Law was given to them by God for
their good; for their protection, physically, practically and
emotionally; and so that they knew how to act in
accordance with what the Father expected from them as
His people. But the Law, as God's representative was
perfect, and man being imperfect, found it impossible to
keep every aspect of the Law. The Law was never meant
to be God's permanent representative on earth to guide
and teach God's people. The Law was only given for a
limited time. The time was coming when a *paidagogos*
would no longer be required....

When the time set by the Father had fully come, God
sent His Son Jesus to be His second representative on the

earth. He came to demonstrate the Father's heart; and He came to redeem us, and to satisfy the perfect demands of the Law by taking the punishment for sin, our sin, every man's sin, upon Himself. All the sin of the whole world, every wrong doing, every crime that would ever be committed, throughout time immemorial, was taken into account. Jesus took the punishment for every sin you can think of - on behalf of us all! He died to sin - once - for all of us - in every generation. Therefore there was no need for the Law anymore because the punishment for every sin man would commit had taken place and the One who was held accountable was dead. He had taken the consequences of mankind's sin upon Himself on the cross; and then when He died He took that sin with Him - into death.

Then, as we know, Jesus was gloriously resurrected three days later. The old had passed away, and the new had come. Jesus had made the way for us, for mankind, to receive a new life that has its source 'in Him' - provided we are prepared to exchange our old life that has its source 'in sin'.

'For He made Him who knew no sin [to be] sin for us, that we might become the righteousness of God in Him.' 2 Corinthians 5:21 (NKJV)

Without the need for the Law anymore, the way was open for the New Covenant of grace to come into operation, the gift of unmerited favour. It meant we were no longer subject to the Law of the Old Testament, no longer under its control. We no longer need that strict *paidagogos*, telling us what to do as he would an underage child or a slave. Instead, through faith in Christ, His born again children have been placed in the privilege position of being a son by adoption.

When Jesus came to earth He demonstrated the Father's love in front of men. But when He returned to His Father, the Holy Spirit was sent as the Father's third and final representative - directly into our hearts. He is the One who calls out *'Abba,* Father' from deep within us. His 'job' is to help us and guide us through relationship, not by written words or by outward demonstration; but by putting His New Covenant law in our minds and by writing it on our hearts   (Jeremiah 31:33 & Hebrews 10:16). The New Covenant is not like the Law, which included the myriad of other laws that came alongside the Ten Commandments. The New Covenant has only two 'laws' and they are - that we love God and we love one another (Jn13:34). These two stipulations take care of everything that we, as believers in Christ, need for life and for relationship with both God and man.

As an adopted son we no longer need to follow the rules imposed from without. We have the Holy Spirit within; and we have freedom to make our own choices, keeping in mind that we are conducting our lives as an adopted son, a representative of our Heavenly Father. If we make wrong choices we can be sure the Holy Spirit within will alert us to that; and be ready to help us to turn around and go in a different direction. Our part is to make sure we don't ignore that check from the Holy Spirit within; or deliberately grieve Him (Ephesians 4:30). Because with His help, we will be able to live our life free from law and condemnation; and we won't find it difficult to please the heart of our Father as His adopted son and heir.

Chapter Eleven

His Letter to the World

As we've seen, when the adult son was chosen by the father for adoption as his son and heir, the official ceremony that took place was made legal under the Law of Adoptia. This meant that the paper work for the adoption would have been sealed, i.e. hot wax would have been dripped on the document and the official seal of the Roman Empire would have been impressed in the hot wax. This official seal made the adoption complete and irrevocable.

'You, yourselves are our letter, written on our hearts, known and read by everybody. You show that you are a letter from Christ, the result of our ministry, written not with ink but with the Spirit of the living God, not on tablets of stone but on tablets of human hearts.' (2 Corinthians 3:2-3).

Having seen all that is involved in our adoption as sons, the significance of the ceremony, and the importance of the seal, it is no wonder that Paul wrote to the Corinthians saying that those who love and follow the Lord Jesus are like a letter. A letter from God to the world, not written by ink but written on our hearts. This human letter, like all official documents has been sealed with a seal - the Father's seal - the Holy Spirit....

'... He anointed us, set his *seal* of ownership on us, and put his Spirit in our hearts as a deposit, guaranteeing what is to come.' 2 Corinthians 1:21-22

How amazing is that! We are His letter to the world, His message has been written on our hearts by the Spirit of the living God. And to confirm the truth of that we have the Father's seal, the Father's 'signature' impressed upon our lives. Like any document authorised in the Roman Empire, or even today in our own legal system, His seal makes what has been written on our hearts and lives official - and it makes it unchangeable and irrevocable. As His letter to the world we just need the confidence to step out, to love people and to let our life reveal that message that comes from Him to them via us. Remembering it's not something that we have to work at, it's who we are - officially!

Waiting Eagerly - Walking in Authority

'Now faith is confidence in what we hope for and assurance about what we do not see.' Hebrews 11:1

It takes faith for us to live as a member of the Father's family; and as a member of His Kingdom. Hebrews tells us clearly - 'Without faith it's impossible to please Him' (Hebrews 11:6). One day, as a young Christian, praying constantly for my unsaved husband, I asked God for a word of encouragement from the Bible. Now I have very rarely been given chapter and verse over the years, but this time I was. However when I looked it up, instead of reading a 'yes he's going to be saved' type of encouragement, what I read was - 'We walk by faith, not by sight' (2 Corinthians 5:7). Father knew that rather than a quick answer to prayer, I needed to grow and develop my faith. Faith that would be strong enough to see the answer to, not just my husband's salvation, but to many more prayer projects to come. It is important to receive answers to our prayers of faith. But it is also important to walk in the assurance and authority that faith builds up.

There are several foundation blocks that faith has already placed into our lives. Right in the beginning, at our new birth, we were saved through faith (Ephesians 2:8). This activated His grace so that our hearts were, and continue to be purified and sanctified by faith (Acts 15:9; 26:18). We are justified by faith and made righteous by faith (Acts 3:28; 4:13). We access His grace and receive the promises of God by faith (Romans 5:2 & Galatians 3:14); and we advance God's work by faith (1 Timothy 1:4). All this in the presence of the many witnesses that surround us; and being spurred on by all that has been accomplished by the men and women of faith that are listed in Hebrews chapter eleven.

In his letter to the Ephesians Paul tells us that - 'God raised us up with Christ and seated us with Him in the heavenly realms in Christ Jesus, in order that in the coming ages He might show the incomparable riches of His grace, expressed in His kindness to us in Christ Jesus.' (Ephesians 2:6-7). This statement is written in the past tense and therefore shows that it has already been done. It's a done deal as they say. But because we obviously aren't seated with Christ physically right now, it means that this 'done deal' has to have been accomplished spiritually and not physically. That means we can only understand that we have been seated with Him in the heavenly realms - by faith alone - we can't see it. Similarly, just as we are seated with Christ in heavenly realms in our spirits, so we have been adopted as His sons and heirs - in our spirits. Our adoption may not have been seen or witnessed by other people in a legal transaction; or by our relocation from one household to another. But that does not in any way diminish the truth that it has been already accomplished - spiritually. For now we 'walk by faith and not by sight' but one day, as the book of Romans tells us, our adoption as His sons and heirs will be seen in all its fullness; both spiritually and in our redeemed bodies.....

'We know that the whole creation has been groaning as in the pains of childbirth right up to the present time.
Not only so, but we ourselves, who have the firstfruits of the Spirit, groan inwardly as we wait eagerly for our adoption to sonship, the redemption of our bodies.'
Romans 8:22-23

When our bodies are redeemed from this corrupt world, whether through death or through the return of Christ at the end of time, our adoption will be fully known and fully expressed. In the meantime, while we wait for that great day, we have the Holy Spirit to help us, as we endeavour to live in the good of all that has taken place in our spirit.

'But if we hope for what we do not yet have, we wait for it patiently.' Romans 8:25

When Jesus walked this earth in His physical body, knowing He was the Son of His heavenly Father, He kept His focus on who His Father was, not on the frailty of His physical and emotional being. He did what He did knowing that He had His Father's delegated authority, just as if He was the Father Himself. We too can do the same if we focus on who the Father is; knowing that we too have been given the Father's delegated authority. Because according to His word - we have been adopted as His sons and heirs.

'But when the fullness of time had come, God sent forth His Son, born of a woman, born under the law, to redeem those under the law, that we might receive the adoption as sons.
And because you are sons, God has sent forth the Spirit of His Son into your hearts, crying out, "Abba Father!"
Therefore you are no longer a slave, but a son, and if a son, then an heir of God through Christ.' Galatians 4:4-7

'Very truly I tell you, whoever believes in me will do the works I have been doing, and they will do even greater things than these, because I am going to the Father.' John 14:12

So how does this delegated authority work? Well it is breathed into us and flows out of us because the Spirit of God has anointed us - 'The Spirit of the Lord GOD is upon me because the LORD has anointed me....' (Isaiah 61:1). In my lexicon/dictionary there is a description of Who the Spirit of God is and what He does on our behalf as Ruach H'Qadosh the Holy Breath of God. Not only does He breathe new life into us and bring us to new birth, He inspires prophecy, instructions and warnings; He endows us with various gifts; He is the energy of life (and therefore relationship); He is manifested in the

Shekinah glory and is never referred to as a depersonalised force. But in particular I was struck by this, in the description of what He does in us and through us- 'imparting warlike energy and executive and administrative power'! This, to me sums up what our adoption as sons is all about. It is to equip us to act like sons on behalf of their Father, in vigorously taking the authority He has given us so that we can execute His will on earth as it is in heaven.

Finally

As you've read this book I hope it has helped you to understand the difference between our modern concept of adoption and the adoption that is written about in scripture. As His born again children, if we can fully grasp what being adopted really means, that we were chosen by our Father and placed in the position of being His son and heir, it will empower us to live our lives with confidence. It will make us aware that it doesn't matter what our previous status in life was, or still is; or whether we are male or female. Those are not the relevant issues.

The bottom line is that we have been chosen as those who can be trusted and given His authority. His seal of authority has been impressed upon our lives and nothing He has decreed about us can be made invalid, changed or reversed. He has become our new Patria Potestas and He has placed us in the irrevocable position of being a joint heir with His Son, Jesus Christ, Jesus the Anointed One.

As Christ....ians, as His sons and heirs, we are not only seated with Christ in heavenly places, we have also been given the authority to go about our Father's business here on earth. We don't need a letter to confirm who we are and to say that we have His authority. We are His letter; and we have been sealed with our Father's signet ring - sealed with the Holy Spirit of God.

TWO MORE BOOKS FROM THE SAME AUTHOR:

The Jewish Wedding and the Bride of Christ

Paperback ISBN: 978-0-9566249-2-5
Kindle eBook ISBN: 978-0-9566249-3-2

'For I have betrothed you to one husband, to Christ, so that I might present you as a pure virgin to him.' 2 Corinthians 11:2

There are many things that Jesus spoke about or referred to that we don't fully understand because they were spoken to people of another culture, and in a context that is not relevant. In this book Mo unravels the deep symbolism of the traditional Jewish wedding and its parallel through Scripture. As the Bible's marriage metaphor is revealed, we are swept up into the sacred romance, discovering how our heavenly Father has sent His holy Matchmaker to find the perfect bride for His beloved Son. This book will teach you, inspire you and enrich your relationship with Jesus. The chapters include:

The Matchmaker
The Bride Price
The Dowry
The Betrothal Ceremony - under the 'chuppah'
The Cup
The Blessing
The Ring, and much more....

How To Pray When He Doesn't Believe' by Mo Tizzard

Paperback ISBN: 978-0-9566249-0-1
Kindle eBook ISBN: 978-0-9566249-1-8

"It's God or me!"

That was the ultimatum Mo faced when she told her husband she had become a Christian. It was the beginning of a time of great pressure and discord in their marriage, but also a time of incredible learning about how to pray and live with her husband under the guidance of the Lord.

Each chapter of the book gives a part of Mo's story, plus principles of prayer based on scriptural teaching. This book offers authentic encouragement to every woman who is married to an unbeliever. Mo speaks into the real issues, in practical ways, as only someone who has 'walked the walk' can do.

The prayers and insights in this book are designed to be helpful, not only for those with unsaved husbands, but for anyone praying for unsaved loved ones or friends. Not only that, many have testified to how this book has encouraged them in praying for their 'prodigals' to come home.

The chapters include:

Increasing Our Faith Level
The Pray and Wait Tactic
Counting the Cost
Discerning God's Opportunities

I Don't Think I Love My Husband Anymore
The Importance of Praise
Removing Hindrances
Cutting the Strings

Plus there is a chapter called 'His Side of Things', which reveals what was going on in Mo's husband, and how he was thinking, during the time she was praying for his salvation.

Because it addresses a need that affects believers in any nation, Mo's book has been translated by foreign publishers into French, Czech, Korean, Russian and into Portuguese for believers in Brazil.

Both the above books can be purchased as a paperback from Amazon in Europe or by emailing storehousebooks@sky.com from outside Europe.
They can also be purchased in eBook form worldwide from any Amazon website.